# Contemporary
# Marketing Research

Dr. A. B. Rao

VISHWAKARMA
PUBLICATIONS VP

# Contemporary Marketing Research

First Edition – June 2015
© Author

**ISBN 978-93-83572-88-5**

**Published by:**
**Vishwakarma Publications**
283, Budhwar Peth, Near City Post,
Pune 411 002.
Phone No: 020 24448989 / 20261157
Email: info@vpindia.co.in
Website: www.vpindia.co.in

Cover Design, Typeset and Layout
**Gold Fish Graphic, Pune.**

Printed by

**Repro India Limited,**
Mumbai

# *Preface*

This book has been written in accordance with the syllabus requirements of the subject " Contemporary Marketing Research" prescribed by the Savitribai Phule Pune University for the MBA Second Year, Sem II.

Lucid and precise explanations along with numerical examples are the important features.

My sincere thanks to the publishers.

**Dr. A. B. Rao**

# Contents

## Appendices

# Detailed Index

## Appendices 173

# Introduction to Marketing Research

The concept of marketing research can be understood in terms of the words marketing and research. It is an appropriate scientific combination of the different processes and activities involved in marketing and in research. Marketing is actually the performance of business activities relating to the goods and services from the producer to the consumer or user. Marketing comprises of production of quality products or provision of standard services. The production has to be in conformity with the requirements of consumers. Product should fetch reasonable profits to the producer. However, it is necessary to see that there is proper link between the important features of quality product, appropriate service, satisfaction of the consumer and justifiable profits. Hence marketing is an essential activity leading to the ultimate human satisfaction of wants.

Research is a search for new knowledge about any defined area over and above the existing knowledge. Research arises out of necessity or curiosity. Research begins with insight hunt of an inquisitive mind. A desire to seek, discover, invent and innovate leads through enquiry and investigation thereby paving the way for research. Research is methodical earnest urge to probe. To explore and acquire more and more of knowledge is the inbuilt disposition of humans. This desire is activised and enthused through scientific mode of thinking, of re-understanding and examining in a better light with a searching eye for new things hitherto unknown. This human quest for understanding is as old as civilization itself. The quest in marketing research is essentially based on an appropriate interlinking of activities relating to marketing functions and as well as research enquiries and processes.

"According to the American Marketing Association, the definition of marketing is as under: Marketing research is the function which links the consumer, customer and public to the marketer through information, information used to identify and define marketing opportunities and problems. Generate, refine and evaluate marketing actions; monitor marketing performance and improve understanding of market as a process. Marketing research specifies the information required to address these issues, designs the method for collecting information; manages and implements the data collection process; analyses the results and communicates the findings and their implications"

The above definition implies that the marketing research activity is essentially based on appropriate and a systematic collection of facts and figures and analysis of the same for the purpose of enabling the marketer to take the right decision.

It is necessary to know the following characteristics of marketing research:

1) It is concerned with the collection, recording, analysis and interpretation of appropriate information relating to the specific product area or service function.

2) The research activities relate to the systematic collection of appropriate details from various relevant sources.

3) Marketing research provides the marketing personnel with useful guidelines relating to goods and services that would satisfy the needs of the consumers.

Marketing research has to be distinguished from market research, in the sense that marketing covers various aspects relating to products and services of different markets. Market therefore is a section of marketing activity. Market research is specific to a part of marketing research, whereas marketing research comprises of all the concerned activities relating to product information and design, product quality, pricing and distribution. Also marketing research deals with various trade channels, sales, promotional advertising and after sales services. Marketing research is oriented towards the building up of consumers confidence in regard to the various products of their consumption. Generally marketing research comprises of the following elements: product research, sales research, advertising research, economic research, packaging research and quantitative export research.

## Scope of Marketing Research:

In the modern times of technological advancement, markets have become more dynamic, competitive and consumer focused. The vision of the manufacturer or service provider is geared towards the fulfillment of the consumers predetermined desires and aspirations in regard to their expectations from the products or services. The scope of marketing research in modern times is quite extensive. Marketing research aims at solving the various problems arising out of various values in accordance with the critical judgements and interpretation of the consumers. Problems that arise in marketing research generally are concentrated around various marketing policies, methods and techniques, channels of distribution, quality channels of products and the different competitive markets. Marketing research helps the marketer to gain competitive advantage. Furthermore, progressive and constant promotion of the brand and also the development of brand consciousness among consumers is an essential objective of the market researcher. Further the researcher has to provide guidelines in regards to publicity, advertising and sales promotion. Various studies relating to the performance of competitive products and their performances have to be undertaken by the researcher.

## Importance of Market Research:

If research is conducted with reference to some specific market or markets, then such research is called market research and it is concerned with the following aspects:

i)      Various classes or types of consumers relating to the existing markets or potential markets and the respective segments,

ii)     In an entire market, the researcher should find the available segments,

3

iii) The varicus purchasing behavioral tendencies of the consumers and their consumption habits and patterns,

iv) The locations of the concerned markets and their respective sizes in the local areas or the global areas i.e, indigenous or overseas markets(International markets),

v) The different positions of supplies of the products in the respective markets,

vi) The growth prospects of the different markets along with their corresponding details of planning,

vii) On the domestic front and as well as on the foreign markets front, the researcher should ascertain and judge the competitive strenghts of the existing competitors. In particular it is necessary to determine the competitive advantage of the manufacturers pertaining to various indigenous products and their markets,

viii) Sharp vision on the part of the market research department is essential to visualize the competitive advantage of the expected new competitive market suppliers,

ix) Scope for improvement in the methods of distribution pertaining to various channels should be appropriately determined,

x) It is imperative to acquire proper technological information and scientific knowledge relating to the prevailing markets,

xi) Market research should evalute the effectiveness of the present promotional aspects and also publicity procedures and the media and as well as the thrust on the advertising front. Also it is necessary to know various technological innovations and the likely changes in the urban liestyles and their effects on the emerging demands for new products.

## Marketing Information System:

Marketing Information System is concerned with the collection of the appropriate information relating to various markets for various products in a scientific and systematic manner so as to facilitate the process of taking decisions by the concerned marketing managers in their respective areas of marketing management. Marketing research provides information that enables the marketing department to store the same and provide it to the concerned marketing managers at the right time, so as to enable them to carry out the right action. A Marketing Information System should be appropriate and useful enough to determine beforehand the information requirements of the marketing departments in the concerned organizations. Marketing Information System generally involves the following types of information: recurrent, monitoring and requested (requisitioned). Information relating to customer satisfaction, sales, advertising expenditures, etc. if supplied on weekly, monthly or on a specified periodical basis then it is called recurrent. Whereas, information that is provided from well defined sources such as companie's annual reports, journals or publications is termed as monitoring information. However, information that is requisitioned or requested is very much concerned with analysis of various competitive products and their prices. Also qualitative testing of the different products and their analysis can also be reckoned as requested information that is sought by the marketing departments.

Marketing information system activity is centralised whereas there exists marketing decision support system which is more or less decentralized and enables marketing managers to deal with related data. The marketing decision support system is categorised into: data management, data sources, display modelling after statistical analysis. For marketing decision support system there can be internal and external sources. Internal sources relate to a company's internal data from its various departments. Whereas, external sources relate to secondary data consisting of published records, reports, periodicals etc. Further secondary data may relate to customer preferences, various retail outlets and their sales, different advertising campaigns etc.

## The procedure for marketing research:

The following are the different steps that can be taken for carrying out marketing research activity:

1) Problem identification and formulation.

2) Marketing information system and the methodology of obtaining the information.

3) The actual procedure adopted for collecting information from various sources.

4) The sampling methodology to be adopted for collecting the required information.

5) Analysis and interpretation of the collected data.

6)     Preparation of marketing research report.

7)     The marketing research report should especially provide guidelines covering the following:

    i)   Research on products and services

    ii)  Research on various markets

    iii) Research on various sales policies and procedures.

## Uses and limitations of marketing research

1)     Marketing research is useful for the main purpose of providing consumer's satisfaction in accordance with the consumers' preferences. Further it is very useful in harmonizing the supply and demand factors. It provides ample guidance for the production of goods that are marketable and that can be distributed appropriately so as to achieve the target of sales and at the same time satisfying the demand requirement.

2)     Marketing research is concerned with the product quality, its precise design, its pricing and also the promotional activities through vigorous advertising so as to gain consumer confidence and establish goodwill.

3)     Through marketing research various products can gain prominence in regard to their well established product brands

In spite of all the above 3 uses there exist certain limitations such as the following,

  a)  Marketing research is not considered by certain critics as necessary because in their view marketing research may not prove to be realistic and appropriately market oriented. It is considered superficial and faulty.

  b)  Marketing research does not provide an overall perspective of a marketing problem .In other words marketing problem cannot be analysed from various approaches. It is considered to be not a totally defectless approach.

  c)  It is very often observed that there may not exist proper concurrence between the marketing research teams and the marketing management personnel in certain marketing aspects in regard to their products. The marketing department may fail to adhere to the guidelines provided by the marketing research department and as a result marketing research activitiy may turn to be futile and wasteful. In short, marketing department may consider itself to be more practical and that their marketing research team's activity as purely theoretical.

## Process of research

In general the process of research can be explained in the following ten steps:

1) **Selection of the Problem Area:** The criteria for the selection of the problem area may depend on any of the following:

(a) Vital or sustaining interest or due to emotional factors.

(b) Search for the best possible solutions to problems in the area of one's own specialisation.

(c) Various contributions that can be helpful.

(d) Feasibility in regard to time, cost and the availability of funds, competence and skills for quantitative data analysis.

2) **Familiarity with the Current Theory and Research:** The existing frontiers of knowledge relating to the problem ,with reference to all the available sources of information and wide literature should be fully understood

3) **Formulation of the Problem and Statement of Objectives:** Statement of the problem should be well articulated so as to be clear and concise .Care should be taken in using the words precisely in accordance with the essential substance of the objectives,

4) **Formulation of the Hypothesis:** Hypothesis is a conjectural statement concerning the possible relationship between two or more variables or inter-connected facts. Hypothesis incorporates questions of fact.

5) **Research Methodology and Sources of Data:** The methodology of research should indicate the appropriate methods. The collected data should be meaningful in accordance with the objectives and hypothesis. Data may be primary or secondary. It should be organised, analysed and used as the basis for decision-making.

6) **Instruments for Collection of Data:** These consist of questionnaires and schedules for conducting the survey and pilot studies.

7) **Validating the Instruments:** Research design and scaling techniques should be clearly explained.

8) **Formal Acquisition of the data:** Collection of the data- practical procedures should be adopted.

9) **Analysis and Findings:** There should be a sense of purpose as well as direction. Findings should be appropriate in accordance with the analysis.

10) **Interpretation and Conclusions:** Generalisations should be realistic and practicable .Implications and action for further research. Conclusions should cover answered as well as unanswered questions.

## Exercise I

**Questions:**

1. What is marketing research?

2. Distinguish between market research and marketing research?

3. Explain briefly the characteristics of marketing research?

4. Explain the scope of marketing research?

5. Explain the importance of market research?

6. What is marketing information system?

7. Explain briefly the importance of marketing decision support system?

8. Explain the procedure for marketing research?

9. Describe the uses and limitations of marketing research?

10. Describe the different steps in the process of research?

11. State whether the following statements are true or false.

   (i) Research is a search for knowledge.

   (ii) Marketing research is the function which provides the consumer, customer and public for marketing information.

   (iii) Marketing research is concerned with the recording and reporting of information only

   (iv) Marketing research provides the marketing personnel with useful guidelines relating to goods and services.

   (v) Market research is concerned with the growth prospects of the different markets.

12.  Fill in the gaps with the appropriate word:

(i)   The sampling methodology is _____ for collecting the necessary information.

a) used  b) required  c) necessary  d) unnecessary

(ii)  Marketing research relates to problem identification and _____.

a) conclusion.  b) formulation  c) statement  d) notification

(iii) The purpose of marketing research is to provide consumer satisfaction in accordance with his/her _____.

a) requirements  b) desires  c) preferences  d) abilities

(iv)  Data should be collected in accordance with _____ and hypothesis

a) needs  b) requirement  c) problems d) objectives

(v)   Statistical data can be collected by using

a) books  b) journals  c) questionnaires  d) surveys

# Marketing research design

## Planning for marketing research

Marketing Research can be carried out for finding solutions to a number of marketing problems. Some of these may relate to :

1.  Sales management, quality, quantity, type of personnel and their training. This includes the efficiency and effectiveness of sales organisation and personnel.

2.  Customer relations service.

3.  Advertising and sales promotion, media research and consumer motivation.

4.  Marketing information systems.

5.  Product standardization and control.

6.  Channels of distribution.

7.    Marketing research relating to sales forecast, industrial and economic forecast.

8.    Marketing policies relating to pricing.

For any type of systematic and scientific research study relating to a marketing phenomena, it is necessary to prepare a plan of action in the form of a 'Research Design'. Research designs are devised in accordance with the objectives of the required marketing research. In other words, 'Research Design' is an appropriately prepared plan of the right action to achieve marketing success. Success results when sales soar high with good profits, consumers express high satisfaction and product gains recognition and acceptance in the minds of the consumers and thereby 'Brand' gets well established. Further, the fundamental requisite is proper marketing knowledge based on continuous research in regard to the dynamic forces of marketing. Marketing knowledge is power and this power of the marketer begets success. Research in marketing should progressively move ahead in accordance with the changing times of the competitive marketing challenges. It is necessary to arrive at new strategies based on new findings and innovations relating to the products of the concerned company or companies. It would be interesting to note certain statements that we come across in 'Economic Times' with news headings such as 'Nestle gives a boost to skincare biz with $ 1.4 b Valeant Deal' (ET dated 29/5/14) and 'Colgate India MD Bets Big on Innovations to Drive Growth' (ET 30/5/14).

Statements of the type stated above arise out of innovative research, vision and foresight of the respective companies. Generally marketing strategies arising out of appropriates research involve the selection of the target product and the choice of the mode of its entry into the target market. For this purpose a proper marketing plan to penetrate into the target market has to be drafted. Also the necessary control systems to be adopted for monitoring the target markets have to be planned.

## Scientific Method

At present due to the competitive tendencies among marketers and also due to changing lifestyles among consumers and also due to the impact of new technological product innovations we do notice the necessity on the part of the marketing research personnel to be more scientific in their assumptions with regard to the changing tastes and preferences as a result of the emotional influences. Scientific method for judging the values and preferences becomes imperative. Scientific method is based on the following three important features:

a) Critical discrimination

b) Generality and system

c) Empirical verification

The main characteristics of scientific method can be stated as

i) **Verifiability**: The conclusion drawn through a scientific method is subjected to verification. Verifiability pre-supposes that the phenomenon must be capable of being measured. This will bring greater accuracy to our verification. For instance, let us consider the famous scientific law that all matter expands on being heated. Now in order to verify this statement we can heat any matter and see whether it has expanded or not. Again the rate of expansion is not the same. Gas expands more than water. Thus, from the general theory that all matter expands on being heated we can proceed to find out the exact degree of expansion.

ii) **Generality**: Scientific laws are universal in their application. Science is not concerned with individual objects or individual groups of objects as such. It is primarily concerned with the types, kinds or classes of objects and events of which the individual objects or events are treated merely as a specimen.

Complete universality is only a myth and is rarely achieved in social science. This is mainly due to heterogeneous nature of social phenomena.

iii) **Predictability**: The result may be predicted with sufficient accuracy. For example, we can say with certainty that if temperature of water is reduced to zero degree it will change into ice. Predictability is based on fixity of relationship between cause and effect and the stability of causative factors themselves.

Predictability thus depends upon the nature of phenomena and our knowledge of various causative factors. Accurate prediction is based on a careful study of various factors.

iv) **Objectivity**: The first requisite of all basic knowledge is the ability to get at the real facts and not to be influenced by notions and own wishes. The main criterion is that all should arrive at the same conclusion about the phenomena, eg. when we say milk is white it is an objective phenomenon.

Objectivity is essential for verification and it permits repetition of observation under identical conditions. This facilitates the verification of observation.

v) **System**: It pertains to the method of arriving at the result. The scientific conclusion is not only true but is based on a systematic mode of investigation. It is only under proper circumstances the results can be verified. In every science there is an accepted mode of investigation and inference which must be adhered to. A haphazard method is not scientific.

## Research design

Planning is an important aspect in regard to the commencement of any type of research investigation. A proper plan of action consisting of the objectives of the investigation, the hypothesis to be examined and the various methods to be adopted for collecting primary data, will have to be prepared. Such a plan provides an outline for the research work to be undertaken and also the nature of analysis of data that has to be carried out. A plan of action is called a research design. The main objective in preparing research design is to enable a researcher to conserve his resources of time, money and energy for the main purpose of reaching the goals of research without any deviation from the main objective.

Thus, a research design can be defined as an outline that provides the specifications for the careful collection of relevant data and appropriate analysis so as to fulfil the objectives of research with precision, economy and perfection.

It is necessary to adhere to the following rules while planning research design:

1. The nature and scope of the problem of research has to be clearly and unambiguously stated. Further, the problem should be of a practical nature in terms of time, money and energy. Further, the validity and reliability of the various conclusions and findings should be pragmatic and verifiable.

2. For the purpose of collection of data, various sources of primary data and the methods that may consist of direct personal investigation, indirect oral investigation, by questionnaire and schedules and also from local sources etc. should be clearly mentioned. In case secondary data is used, the nature of the authenticity should be stated for the purpose of the verification of the same if deemed necessary by any scrutinizer. If data is

to be collected through a survey by questionnaire, then the nature of the questions should be explained.

3.  The hypothesis or hypotheses should be in consonance with the objectives of the research. The nature of the research methods and their appropriateness for the purpose of study should be explained. The research methodology and the type of research should be clearly stated.

4.  The reason for selecting a particular time period relating to the problem of study should be clarified. The geographical limits depending upon the problem should be stipulated.

5.  The nature of the sampling design that would be adopted should be explained. The adequacy of the sample and the sampling errors, if any, should be also be mentioned.

6.  In the case of research pertaining to a business or managerial problem, the background along with various aspects of the problem to be investigated should be explained. In the case of research pertaining to a problem in pure sciences, the appropriate scientific methods and experimental methods and methodology to be used, should be stated. With reference to problems of social research, it is necessary to state the relevance and necessity and the social context for the investigation.

7.  In the case of social research it is necessary to mention which particular forms of research design amongst the following have been selected.

    a)  Single Design

    b)  Classical Design

    c)  Comparison Design

    d)  Experimental Design

The qualitative aspect in the choice of the design has to be explained.

## Necessity for Research Design

1.  Research design enables a researcher to chart out his course of action in accordance with an overall picture of the various aspects of his research problem. Thereby, his research operations would become practically amenable and easy.

2.   A researcher can adopt appropriate methodology on the basis of the use of the right techniques and methods. The data collection activity must become orderly and smooth.

3.   Planned and well organized approach leads to the efficiency in the procedure of research and saves much time, money and energy.

4.   A well directed approach on the basis of a perfect design is conducive to the promotion of harmonious functioning of various persons associated with the problem of the research project.

5.   A crystal -clear objective-oriented research design alone can lead to appropriate data analyses by reducing unnecessary wastage of time, money and effort.

6.   Research success is almost and always dependent on a superb design of research.

## Principles of Research Design

The three principles of research design can be stated as replication, randomization and local control.

Replication stands for the number of times each experiment procedure is repeated in an experiment. In short, experimental activity is repeatedly performed for the purpose of ensuring, increasingly the accuracy of the observations and emerging phenomena. Estimations can be made reliable.

Randomization principle enables the researcher to ensure against the influential effects of extraneous factors in the course of experimentation.

The principle of 'local control' is applied for the purpose of elimination of variability that may arise due to the extraneous factors.

These principles of research design are of much importance in conducting agricultural experiments.

## Characteristics of a good research design

1.   A qualitative design of research can be a single design, a comparison design or an experimental design.  It can be a classical design as well. The type of the design is a notable feature for the collection of appropriate information.

2.  An effective design always states the nature of the required facts and figures and various reliable sources for obtaining the same.

3.  A good research design always encourages the researchers to carry out appropriate analysis of data with confidence, thereby leading to reliable and accurate conclusions.

4.  A consistent research design specifically states the nature and explains the purpose of variables such as dependent, independent and extraneous.

5.  A proper experimental design can lead to effective control of extraneous variables in the course of experimentation.

6.  An appropriate design always aims at minimizing the errors that may arise in the performance of an experiment.

7.  A reliable research design provides various details relating to the budget of the research and the overall costs.

8.  A practical research design provides practical and helpful hints and strategies to a researcher for the collection of necessary information.

9.  An important research design always emphasizes on the maximization of the authenticity of the data by stating the precautions to be taken in respect of sampling design and also during the survey process.

10. A relevant research design eliminates irrelevance and promotes the reliability of investigation by the statement of scrupulously planned course of research action.

11. A good research design is characterized by appropriately planned spelled out standards of research performance with an assurance of analysis that can lead to the discovery of hitherto unknown things and ideas.

## Types of Research Design

In accordance with the nature of research studies ,research activity can be designed. Research designs have been categorized under the following three different heads:

1.  Exploratory Research Studies

2.  Descriptive Research Studies

3.  Causal Research Studies

## 1.     Exploratory Research Studies

Research design in case of exploratory research studies is based on the specific nature of the problem of investigation. An exhaustive literature survey concerning the subject matter of investigation is undertaken. The hypothesis framed by earlier researchers are examined, evaluated and reviewed for  new investigations.

This design takes into consideration the views and experiences of some selected respondents. The researcher obtains new details that could help him in the pursuit of his research.

Apart from the above, the researcher can carry out intensive studies by examining certain existing records. He can as well obtain interesting and innovative facts and ideas. In short, he can explore latent and hitherto unknown data.

## 2.     Descriptive Research Studies

Social research is generally of a descriptive nature .Research design takes into account the various aspects of a problem or a situation for the purpose of a detailed, intensive and scrupulous study. Here the research emphasis is on the qualitative or descriptive facts of investigation and not on the quantitative measurement.

The research design states the different stages of the descriptive research. The stages include: the statement of the objectives and hypothesis, data collection; the basis of a questionnaire and interviews; carrying out analysis, interpretation; drawing conclusions and preparing a research report. Here the research design necessarily requires great care and caution for appropriate coverage and thorough study.

## 3.     Causal Research Studies

In regard to any problem of investigative research, a researcher studies the causes and effects so as to predict future trends. Further, he gets an insight as to how to control the effects. The causal relationship between the variables can be studied, when the research design outlines the relevant hypothesis to be tested.

## Research method

Marketing Researchers generally use the following research methods

1)      Field study method

2)      Experimental or laboratory method

3)      Survey method

4)      Case study method

5)      Statistical method

When a marketing research problem has been formulated and also the necessary literature survey has been carried out in accordance with the objectives and hypothesis, then it would be necessary for the researcher to use anyone or an appropriate combination of the above mentioned five methods.

## Field study method

Field study method is adopted for getting information in the form of facts and figures from the persons in the concerned area. The procedures for collecting information consists of:

a)      direct personal interview

b)      indirect oral interview

c)      through questionnaires and schedules

The various aspects relating to the above procedures are explained in the chapter on 'collection of data'

## Experimental and Laboratory method

Experimental type of research is used for conducting enquiries with reference to the product acceptance or rejection. In all investigations pertaining to certain areas such as physics or chemistry or related sciences, experimentation in a laboratory becomes a necessity. Agricultural experiments in regards to yields of various groups are carried out to ascertain the nature of variation in the yields. But in regard to the marketing of products, experiments are carried out with reference to various segments so as to verify the preference variations amongst the segments and also within the segments

## Survey method

Survey method is used in the areas of social sciences, commerce and management. In regard to marketing, the survey method depends on the views and opinions of various groups of consumers. On the basis of a research design and sampling design, a well structured questionnaire is used for collecting the product or service details from the concerned respondents. If the researcher or enumerator goes to the place of the respondents and while interviewing the concerned persons, fills in the questionnaire, then such questionnaires are termed as 'schedules'. Surveys are useful in obtaining the past and as well as present details. Researcher can usually predict certain results to some reliable extent. But the success of this method depends on the appropriate size of the representative sample, sampling methodology and the authenticity of the information provided by the respondents.

## Case study method

This is a useful method for the study of a problem on the basis of the characteristics of aspects relating to the given problem. These aspects may deal with a particular situation or a happening. A case study may be characterized by certain preferences or likes and dislikes of the respondents in an environment of enterprising competitors. When compared with other methods this method has the following distinct features:

i)      The individual unit of study pertains to an unknown population.

ii)     The characteristics of the case are carefully studied, described and explained.

iii)    Inferences are drawn in accordance with the context of the case and also on the basis of similar cases.

## Statistical method

This method relates to the study of the quantitative aspects involved in a problem relating to a group of products and their competitors. For the purpose of analyses certain statistical techniques for testing hypothesis are used. Parametric or non-parametric tests of significance may also be used depending upon the relevance and applicability. The advantage of statistical methodology is that precise and logically consistent conclusions can be drawn. However, as marketing research is more concerned with the behavioural tendencies of the consumers it is necessary to take proper care to ensure that error free, qualitatively meaningful and quantitatively reliable conclusions are arrived at.

## Hypothesis

Every type of enquiry has to begin with some basic, sensible propositions or suppositions. A proposition is made from some known facts for the purpose of logical reasoning or scientific investigation. A supposition or proposition is termed as 'Hypothesis'. If more than one hypotheses is framed, then we consider all such framed statements as hypotheses. The following is an example of a hypothesis: "Banks are shaping up, consolidating and venturing out into insurance business in a significant way." Hypothesis can be classified as

i. Working hypothesis

ii. Research hypothesis

iii. Scientific hypothesis

iv. Statistical hypothesis consisting of Null hypothesis and Alternate hypothesis

## Explanations

**Working hypothesis:** When a researcher assumes temporarily certain facts in the course of his preliminary study of a problem, then he may make a tentative proposition that is not final. Such a course of action makes him frame a working hypothesis.

**Research hypothesis:** It arises out of the finalization of a working hypothesis.

**Scientific hypothesis:** When a hypothesis is framed, on the basis available, adequate data, for the purpose of empirical verification and systematic justification, then it becomes a scientific hypothesis.

**Statistical hypothesis:** These are propositions that express quantitative relationships. A statistical hypothesis comprises of Null hypothesis and Alternate hypothesis. When the researcher is interested in finding the existence or non existence of a quantitative relationship, then he proceeds in an unbiased manner by assuming the non existence of a relationship. Such an assumption is called 'Null Hypothesis'. If he supposes the contrary, i.e., the existence of a relationship, then his hypothesis would be 'Alternate Hypothesis'. If Null hypothesis is accepted as true on the basis of empirical verification, then the

Alternate hypothesis is rejected and vice versa. It is the Null hypothesis that is always tested. For instance, if the average age of the students of division A of a class is denoted by $x1$ and that of division B by $x2$, then the Null hypothesis is expressible as H0: $x1 = x2$ and the alternate hypothesis would be H1: $x1 \neq x2$. Hence the statistical hypothesis would be H0: $x1 = x2$ and H1: $x1 \neq x2$.

## Criteria for a Good Hypothesis

The applicability of statistical hypothesis can be understood with reference to various problems in the hypothesis relating to testing of the hypothesis (7th and 8th chapter). The criteria for a good hypothesis can be stated as follows:

a)      It should possess conceptual clarity and precision.

b)      It should never be framed as a question.

c)      It should be specific, concise and meaningfully worded.

d)      It should not contain contradictory clauses or statements.

e)      A hypothesis can be a statement expressing the relationship between the specified variables.

f )      A hypothesis can be framed as a descriptive statement relating to the pertinent issue of a problem.

g)      A hypothesis relating to problem in a social science must be relevant and scientifically realistic and verifiable.

## Exercise II

**Questions:**

1.  Explain important features of planning for marketing research?

2.  Explain what you understand by Scientific method?

3.  State the characteristics of Scientific method

4.  Do you agree with the statement that scientific method involves critical discrimination, generality and system and empirical verifications. If so state the reasons.

5.  What is research design? Explain

6.  State the principles of research design?

7.  What are the characteristics of a good research design?

8.  Explain the different types of research design

9.  Explain some research methods that are used by the marketing researcher

10. What is a hypothesis?

11. Explain the criteria for a good hypothesis

12. "Marketing research can be more appropriately studied using certain case studies" Comment on the given statement.

13. State whether the following statements are true or false:

    i)   In marketing research, exploratory design is more often used than descriptive or causal.

    ii)  Marketing research success is independent of a good research design

    iii) For framing hypothesis statistically, alternate hypothesis is always necessary.

    iv)  If null hypothesis is true then alternate hypothesis is false.

v) A good research design always aims at minimizing the errors that may arise in the performance of an experiment.

14. Fill in the gaps with the appropriate word:

i) Scientific method aims at clarity and _____.

a) vision b) reason c) precision d) decision

ii) Scientific method is a problem _____ method.

a) finding b) making c) solving d) involving

iii) An important characteristic of science is _____.

a) discrimination b) discretion c) judgement d) comment

iv) A good hypothesis has to be meaningfully _____.

a) explained b) worded c) stated d) mentioned

v) Experimental method may be mainly concerned with product acceptance or _____.

a) refusal b) rejection c) concession d) submission

# Media Research, Data Collection and Questionnaires

## Types of marketing research

Traditional marketing is characterized by certain types of procedures in marketing for the purpose of promotion of products and brands. In modern times there is very much technological impact on the types of marketing research. At present there exist various forms of electronic media and digital marketing or internet marketing which are of much convenience and use for the consumers. Electronic media has tremendous scope to enable the consumer to get access to the right type of information at any place and at any time. The modern times are governed by technological advances in appropriate communication. Internet marketing in terms of various kinds of digital marketing can be used in any of the following forms: Website, online video, email marketing, mobile marketing, blogs, internet banner ads, pay-per-click advertising, social media marketing (Facebook, LinkedIn, Twitter, Pinterest, Tumblr, G+ and so on).

The advantage of the above mentioned types of marketing is that they are modern and can transmit messages to customers at less cost than newspaper, radio, magazine or T.V. ad. Another advantage is that very large audience, anywhere in the globe can be reached.

The traditional marketing has also certain merits. We consider the following types of marketing research for the promotion of marketing of products and services with the ultimate objective of consumer satisfaction. The following important types of marketing research are worth studying.

1) Product Research

2) Consumer Research

3) Distribution Research

4) Media Research

5) Research on test marketing

6) Research on market analysis and sales forecast

1)   **Product Research**: Product research is helpful in identifying various special features and their intrinsic values to all those consumers belonging to a certain segment of the market. Product design takes into consideration the nature of package and the price. Customer acceptance of a product or service is carefully observed and minutely studied in an environment of competitive forces for similar products and services. Product Research necessitates the comparison of the concerned product with similar or related products and their respective prices in the prevailing market in the urban and as well as in the rural areas. Product is the dominant factor necessitating continuous improvement efforts on the path of the manufacturer. The middleman or distributors and consumers and their preferences are keenly met with by the manufacturer. At present, product research is extensively carried out with a special attention to sales volume. The aim of research is to identify the weaknesses in the existing products and overcoming the same by continuous research efforts and improvements. Every manufacturer has

to effectively compete with the leading competitive brands for gaining competitive advantage.

2) **Consumer Research** Next to product is to identify the characteristics of consumer buying behaviour in various market segments. Consumer opinions and views in regard to products of their consumption are always changing with the lifestyles and changing times. Here in this respect, behavioural sciences are of much relevance to market researcher. Brand preference, buying power, disposable income are all important aspects that are researched continuously. Consumer outlook is of paramount attention by every market researcher.

3) **Distribution Research:** There exist various channels of effective distribution. Distribution deals with logistics or facilities that exist for physical distribution. It is necessary to study the relevant outlets and channels of distribution for the purpose of carrying out cost patterns and the related problems concerned with the economic inequalities.

4) **Media Research:** The main objective in carrying out media research is to find out the most appropriate promotional media which may consist of print, tv, e-mail or Internet. Research while catering to consumers needs and satisfaction should also study the cost of promotion and other overheads. Research should ultimately focus on consumer's behaviour without losing the sight on the profits.

5) **Research on test Marketing:** Test marketing is involved with certain steps aiming at ascertaining the extent of marketability of a newly developed product. The following are the usual steps

   i) A manufacturer has to find out or estimate the scale of his new product

   ii) Manufacturer has to select a suitable plant to facilitate the proposed manufacture of the product. This plant is known as pilot plant.

   iii) The objective of the pilot plant is to carry out a marketing test through the identification of a range of marketing activities.

   iv) In other words test marketing aims at carrying out appropriate action on the basis of small scale experimentation relating to manufacture of the concerned product.

v) Test marketing enables a manufacturer to proceed with minimum risk based on a suitably small investment of money, effort and time.

All these steps would ultimately enable a manufacturer to take a decision on a larger scale.

6) **Research on Market Analysis and Sales Forecast**: The traditional method is specially used to collect informative data. Based on the past and the present sales, marketing researcher has to study the following important aspects for promotional purposes:

a) The present position of marketing activity .How far marketing plans have proved to be realistic?

b) In view of the consumers changing needs the producer has to determine the additional financial requirements and work out the cost structure for bringing out the necessary modifications and technological changes in the product. He has also to plan the methodology and strategic changes to be introduced in the manufacturing processes for increasing efficiency in the operations. Market analysis provides a new vision to the companies' managers to counter act effectively the competing tendencies and thereby estimate and forecast progressive sales of their company's products. For the purpose of forecasting, appropriate statistical techniques have to be used.

Through the usage of the appropriate media (digital and as well as traditional) the marketing research process can become a success because managers can deal effectively with the complexity of changing customer relationships across a number of channels. Also marketing research would enable the marketers to meet appropriately with the changing customer interactions. Further practical decisions based on the new and valuable data would become an obvious reality.

## Statistical Enquiry

A statistical enquiry stands for the entire process: collecting measurable information in the form of facts and figures- on all aspects of a problem connected with the object of enquiry, classifying, tabulating and presenting it in the form of graphs, charts and diagrams, analysing and interpreting it, using statistical methodology and drawing inferences and general conclusions. A thorough statistical enquiry has several stages.

Before beginning the actual work of collecting statistical data, it is necessary to know the preliminary requisites for its collection. Since statistical materials are numerical it is important to collect only facts that can be quantitatively measured. Hence only those facts that have quantitative characteristics can come under the domain of statistical collection.

## Object and Scope of a Statistical Enquiry

Object and scope of a statistical enquiry will have to be clearly outlined before undertaking the actual work of collecting data. This enables the investigator to avoid collecting unnecessary and irrelevant data and concentrate only on obtaining information that is directly connected with the object of his enquiry. The most important things to remember while planning an enquiry is that you should obtain the most reliable and maximum information relevant to the purpose of enquiry with the minimum use of time, money and energy.

An enquiry may be either a general-purpose enquiry or a specific- purpose enquiry. For instance, an enquiry regarding the educated unemployed in India, or into the working condition of college teachers in India, has its own set of object and purpose, hence it is specific purposes enquiry. The population census, which is general and exhaustive and is undertaken once in ten years, is a general-purpose enquiry. These enquiries are undertaken at certain regular intervals of time, conditions or circumstances, without materially altering their general structure and purpose.

## Types of Statistical Enquiry

1.  **Original or Non original**: A statistical enquiry that is undertaken for the first time is said to be original. Those that have been undertaken on previous occasions are non original or repetitive. In repetitive types of enquiries, necessary modifications may be made from time to time.

2.  **Census or Sample**: A census enquiry is an all inclusive or exhaustive type, for it takes into consideration details about every member figuring in it. It results, therefore, are likely to be highly dependable and provide an accurate picture of the problem being investigated. But it is costly, time consuming and tiresome. In a sample enquiry on the other hand

only details about some or a few members figuring in it are taken into account. The sample, if carefully and intelligently selected according to sampling principles, not only gives satisfactory results it also saves time, money and energy. The nature of the problem to be investigated itself suggests whether an enquiry should be of the census type or of the sample type.

3.  **Official or Non official**: Enquiries undertaken by or on behalf of central or state governments are known as official enquiries. Those enquiries undertaken by private individuals or institutions with government consent or support are called semi -official enquiries.

4.  **Confidential or Open**: Enquiries that are not to be disclosed to the public are confidential enquiries. All those enquiries, details about which can be made known to the public are open or non-confidential enquiries in ; fact there is nothing confidential about them.

5.  **Direct or Indirect**: A direct enquiry is one which the facts are quantitatively measurable. On the other hand ,an indirect enquiry is one in which the facts cannot be expressed directly in quantitative terms .For instance ,while the income, ages and expenditures of a group of workers can be measured quantitatively ,it is not possible to do that while examining the honesty ,ability and  capacity to work. In dealing with facts that cannot be expressed directly in numerical terms, an indirect type of enquiry has to be undertaken. For instance, the intelligence of a group of students can be gauged from the ability of individual members of the group to answer a given number of difficult questions in the shortest period of time correctly. Their intellectual abilities are determined by the marks they score.

## Internet Marketing

The use of the internet facility and the corresponding digital technologies for the purpose of achieving the required objectives of marketing, is called Internet Marketing. Internet Marketing activities and e business have much in common. This is because electronic commerce includes all those operations relating to online commerce, digital commerce or internet commerce. In modern times of galloping technological advances, internet marketing communication has a significant importance when compared with traditional marketing. This is because digital media through satellite and mobile phones has brought about a definite advantage.

Internet has strategic advantage because it involves customer analysis, supply chain management, competitor analysis and decision making through market analysis and environmental scanning. Internet also accelerates the operational and supportive usage of product promotions through publicity, advertising media and through related logistics and distribution networks.

The advantage of Internet is that it is useful to vary the elements of marketing mix consisting of product, promotion, price, people, processes and place. Further, Internet support for making communication is very essential. Communication may be personal based on direct marketing and video conferencing, whereas impersonal communication involves sales promotion, advertising and public relations.

## Statistical units

Things are measured in one type of unit or another. An exact, precise, clear cut and rigid definition of the unit of measurement is absolutely necessary for accurate, proper and thorough enquiries.

The purpose and scope of the enquiry itself determine the nature of the unit, for instance units of measurement maybe in kilometres, metres, tonnes, quintals, kilograms, grams, litres or hours. These units are well known but sometimes in statistical enquiries we may come across units such as income - earners, accident-crimes all of which need proper and clear cut definitions relevant to the object of the enquiry. Otherwise questions like what type of income - earners? what different types of accidents? and so on arise leading to confusion. Great care and precision must go into the definition of statistical unit. To give another example, if there is an enquiry into the country's educated unemployed it should be carefully defined. Does educated mean matriculates, undergraduates or graduates or all of these? How many months or years must an individual be out of a job to be classified as unemployed? These are the questions that need careful consideration before undertaking the actual enquiry.

Statistical unit should possess these ideal characteristics:

1.       Its definition must be intelligible, clear-cut, rigid and unambiguous.

2.     It should be relevant to the object of enquiry.

3.     It should possess stability and homogeneity and must remain uniform throughout the statistical investigation.

## Kinds of units

**Units of collection or enumeration:** These are the units in terms of which data concerning the field of enquiry are collected. For instance the total production of sugar in India may be measured in terms of lakh metric tonnes, production of cotton cloth in million meters and footwear exports in thousands of pairs. Further, a unit of measurement may be either simple or composite. When a simple unit is qualified by the addition of a qualifying word to it, it becomes a composite unit. For example, foot pounds, passenger kilometres and road accidents are all composite units.

**Units of analysis interpretation and comparison:** For the purpose of comparison and analysis and interpretation of different sets of data units may be expressed as co-efficients, percentages, ratios and rates. In statistical analysis we are concerned with comparing facts in relation to different times, different situations or different conditions. Coefficients and ratios are obtained by comparing two quantities one of which is taken a numerator and another as denominator. Both quantities that are compared must be homogeneous and related to each other. A percentage is a comparison between a variable quantity and 100 (for example 68 is to 100 means 68 percent and is written as 68%). A rate is a comparison between one quantity and another, both of which have some relationship. For instance, the statement that the population of India is increasing by some 3% per annum expresses the rate of increase of population of India as a percentage.

**Accuracy and approximation:** No statistical enquiry can have the stamp of dependability without it being reasonably accurate. Therefore in any kind of statistical investigation, investigators should aim at a high degree of accuracy, in keeping with the fundamental objectives of the investigation. The sum and substance of any statistical enquiry is that it is primarily concerned with ,as far as possible, accurately obtainable results and not necessarily with exact or hundred percent accurate results.

In any statistical enquiry, the degree of accuracy desirable depends on the nature of the problem of enquiry. For example when figures on the annual production of iron and steel in India are to be given, it is sufficient to mention upto  lakh tonnes. On the other hand gold and silver prices need to be quoted upto the last paisa. While measuring the distance between two railway stations it's enough to state it to the nearest kilometre. For instance the distance is : 192 kilometres. Therefore what is desirable in statistical data is a reasonably high degree of accuracy that is best suited to the nature of the data. In other words, accuracy need not be a hundred percent but only to that degree which the nature of the data demands.

Inaccuracies and errors are usually the result of human frailty and defective instruments of measurement. A human being is not a machine that can ensure absolute technical accuracy. Furthermore, the instruments may be defective or wrongly used because of ignorance or carelessness. Therefore achieving nearly perfect results in statistical investigation is possible only through willing efforts towards that end . And even though absolute accuracy can't be assured in any statistical investigation and sometimes may be deemed to be superfluous and undesirable investigators should constantly endeavour to reflect the realities of their investigations by minimising the so-called unavoidable inaccuracies and errors that may knowingly or unknowingly creep into their work.

As far as numerical figures that involve decimal fractions are concerned, the required approximations can be made. Approximations can be made provided sufficient calculations are performed. That is, calculations will have to be made up to 2, 3 or 4 decimal places depending on whether approximations are required up to 1, 2 or 3 decimal places. For instance, consider the figure 23.61862. The approximation to four decimal places is 23.6186. Approximation up to three decimal places is 23.619 and 23.62 upto two decimal places. In making an approximation of any quantity to the required number of decimal places we increase the digit in that place- that is, the required decimal place like the second, third etc.- by one digit if the next digit is equal to five or greater than five. And we leave it unaltered if the next digit is less than 5. For example: 36.805 when reduced to approximately two decimal places becomes 36.81. The figure 36.814 becomes 36.81 while 36.815 is 36.82

## Statistical errors

'Errors' are of much significance in statistics. An error in statistics means the difference between the true or accurate value and the estimated or approximate value. Thus, errors in the statistical sense is not to be confused with 'mistake'.

Errors in statistical data may be in the form of errors of origin, of manipulation, of inadequacy cr of insufficiency. Errors that arise from inaccuracy or prejudice in the collection of data or due to the wrong selection of statistical units are errors of origin. Errors of manipulation occur when persons use approximations, or unconsciously measure, or wrongly count, or use instruments wrongly or manipulate them. Incomplete or insufficient data lead to errors of inadequacy.

Statistical errors can be measured in absolute and relative terms. An 'absolute error' is the difference between the true value and the estimated value of a numerical item, while a 'relative error' is the ratio of the absolute error, to the estimated value of the numerical item. For instance, if the actual profit of a business man are Rs3200 and are estimated at Rs 3000, then the relative error is 200/ 3000= 1/15= 0.6667 and the percentage of error is 6.67.

For the purpose of comparison of errors due to estimation and approximation, relative errors are of more importance than absolute error.

## Classes of errors

There are two main classes of errors: biased errors and unbiased errors

1.   **Biased errors:** these errors are the direct consequences of human weaknesses. Sometimes informants, enumerators or investigators underestimate or overestimate purposely. In other words these errors arise while using instruments of measurements improperly. It is obvious that these errors are cumulative as the number or observations go up, the absolute errors also increase.

2.   **Unbiased errors:** There's always an element of chance in statistical investigation and estimation, so much so that it becomes very difficult to avoid errors- that is, errors without bias. Broadly speaking, unbiased errors are the result of chance, approximations, pure mistakes or slips.

The other classes of errors are possible errors and probable errors.

## Possible errors:

In approximating any quantity, there is always the possibility or an error due to approximation; This is a 'possible error'. For instance, the number 84.163 when expressed correctly to three decimal places may be an approximation of any one of these ten values: 84.1 625, 84. 1626, 84. 1627,  84. 1628, 84. 1629, 84. 1630, 84. 1631, 84. 1632, 84. 1633, 84. 1634.

That is, the number is greater than or equal to 84.1625  but less than 84.1635. Therefore, 84.163 correct to three decimal places = 84.1625+ 0.0005.

The' limits of error' are - 0.0005 and +0.0005. In other words if 84.1625 is called the lower limit then 84.1635 is the upper limit. At the lower limit the possible error is -0.0005 and at the upper limit the possible errors is + 0.0005.

## Probable errors:

This stands for the numerical item which when added to a given quantity and also when subtracted from the same quantity provides the limits within which that quantity may vary. For example if the coefficient of correlation between two variables X and Y is +0.54 and its probable error is 0.01  then the coefficient of correlation will lie between 0.54 -0.01 or + 0.53 and 0.54 + 0.01 or +0.55.

## Collection of data

Collecting reliable and as far as possible accurate data is the fundamental objective of any statistical investigation. The quality and dependability of statistics more or less depend on the method used in their collection. All collected statistics should have an existence and a living reality of their own, otherwise the entire exercise of collection may turn out to be a farce and the statistics may be condemned as 'tissues of falsehood' or 'figments of the imagination'. Therefore if statistics are to be reliable, enumerators, investigators and organisations collecting the data should put in painstaking  efforts, and use reason and common sense.

Statistical data can be divided into primary data and secondary data.

## Primary data

By primary data we mean the data that have been collected originally for the first time. In other words, primary data may be the outcome of an original statistical enquiry, measurement of facts or a count that is undertaken for the first time. For instance, data of population census is primary. Primary data being fresh from the fields of investigation is very often referred to as raw data. In the collection of primary data a good deal of time, money and energy are required.

The following are the methods of collecting primary data:

i)      Collection directly by personal investigation.

ii)     Collection indirectly by oral investigations.

iii)    Collection by questionnaire and schedule.

iv)     Collection from statistical reports of correspondents and from local sources.

**(I)**     **Collection directly by personal investigation**: Statistical data can be collected directly by the investigator by personally approaching the people concerned. This implies that the investigator has to be present on the spot and interview the people. In order to collect reliable data, he has to study thoroughly and closely the problem of his investigation.

The investigator has to make on-the-spot-observations on the customs, traditions, habits and behaviour of the people picturing in the problem of his investigation. This means that for thorough and convincing results, he has to project himself, with all his mind, heart and commonsense, on the living plains of his informants. Further, personal investigation calls for a certain degree of caution and tact on the part of the interviewer since he has to put sensible and unambiguous questions to elicit the required information.

This method of gathering data being of an intensive type, a good deal of time, money, energy and patience are indispensable. Furthermore, success in this type of investigation is largely dependent on the investigator than on the informants, for the investigator should be impartial without an iota of prejudice.

**(II)**    **Collection indirectly by oral investigation**: When it is not possible or is not desired to collect information directly by personal investigation, an indirect method of oral investigation can be carried out.

Enquiry committees and commissions appointed by government, for carrying out certain enquiries and investigations, invariability resort to this method of investigation. According to this method, some persons who in the opinion of the enquiry committee or investigation commission are understood to be in full possession of the knowledge of the facts under investigation and from the information furnished by them, the actual position is ascertained and conclusions are drawn.

Before this type of enquiry is actually undertaken, a list of appropriate questions pertaining to the investigation is prepared.

The accuracy and the success of this method depend upon the type of persons interrogated.

These informants should be of stable disposition neither too optimistic nor too pessimistic, of an even temperament, of good standing, of sound mind, of honest behaviour and lastly, persons who can express their views correctly.

**(III)** **Collecting by Questionnaires and Schedules**: A questionnaire is simply a paper-sheet or a few paper-sheets containing a number of questions printed, typed or cyclostyled. These questions usually are very carefully drafted keeping in view the main objective, nature and scope of the problem under investigation.

Though questionnaires and schedules very often mean the same, yet there exists a subtle difference. Schedules are usually blank forms containing certain blank columns under relevant headings. These schedules are commonly meant to be filled by interviewers or enumerators. Questionnaires are very often supposed to be filled by informants. Filling up a schedule invariably requires some training. Questionnaires are necessary followed by sufficient instructions, as regards the procedure and manner, of answering the questions. When both the methods, direct personal investigation and as well as indirect oral investigation are found too costly, time-consuming or unsuitable for a particular type of investigation, the 'Questionnaire Method' is most advantageously used. As this method has an immense practical significance, its use in many types of enquiries is obviously justifiable.

By means of schedules and questionnaires data can be collected as follows:

**Procedure (a):** By dispatching the questionnaires and schedules to the informants so that they may complete and return the same.

**Procedure (b):** By sending certain officials called enumerators with schedules, so that they (enumerators) may guide the informants in filling up their schedules.

**Procedure (a) explained:** According to this method the questionnaires and schedules are sent through post, for being filled up properly and returned by the informants in time before a specified date. This method is not only expeditious but also comparatively cheap. This plan can be advantageously used when the field of enquiry is vast and implies high cost and a good lot of time and energy, if undertaken according to direct personnel investigation or indirect oral investigation.

While this method has certain advantages it has its obvious drawbacks. If questions are framed unwisely, improperly and carelessly, without the use of courteous expressions wherever necessary and without sufficient degree of tact then it is quite possible that the individuals concerned may not care to answer them or may be prejudiced or resentful. Even if some furnish information, they may furnish unwanted and incorrect information. Moreover, some individuals by not returning them may safely deposit them in the dustbin. This method can be highly advantageous only when it has the force of a law behind it.

**Procedure (b) explained:** If officials are sent to guide and help the informants in filling up the questionnaires and schedules, then the results would be quite encouraging. If further the officials explain to the informants the object, scope and practical utility of their enquiry, then the informants may not only become interested in the enquiry and co-operate accordingly, but they may be too eager to answer the questions. It is therefore necessary that the officials should be trained in human psychology and also in the manner of approaching the people. Success in this method of investigation is largely dependent upon the abilities of the enumerators and investigators.

## The Essentials of a Good Questionnaire

While drafting a good questionnaire, the following points should be borne in mind:

1. Questions should be simple, brief and few in number.

2. Questions should be free from ambiguity, easily intelligible and readily answerable.

3. Questions should be such that they can be answered by a 'yes' or 'no' or merely by a number.

4. They should be framed tactfully without either calling for confidential information or arousing feelings of resentment or irritation.

5.  Questions should be generally corroboratory in nature to the extent possible.

6.  Questions should be capable of directly eliciting the desired information without prejudice on the part of the informants.

7.  Whenever necessary, desirable and possible, the questions should be courteously worded so as to carry an appeal and not show any force of compulsion.

(IV) **Collection from Statistical Report of Correspondent and from Local Sources:** Sometimes, certain facts may be incapable of exact measurement or complete enumeration or it may not be considered necessary to undertake detailed enumeration. In such cases it may be possible to obtain approximate results or estimates. When such approximate results on estimates are considered quite sufficient for the purpose of certain enquiries, then the data collecting organisations may ask certain local agents or correspondents to send in reliable and most appropriate estimates

The chief advantage of this method is that it is not costly and at the same time proves to be quite expeditious Therefore this method of collection can be used whenever quick estimates or approximate results are desired and deemed to be quite adequate.

## Secondary Data

Secondary data are the data that are in actual existence in accessible records, having been collected and treated statistically by the persons maintaining the records. In other words, secondary data are the data that have been already collected, presented, tabulated, treated with necessary statistical techniques and conclusions have been drawn. Therefore, collecting secondary data doesn't mean doing some original enumeration but it merely means obtaining data that have already been collected by some agencies, reliable persons, government departments, research workers, dependable organisations etc. Secondary data are easily obtainable from reliable records, books, government publications and reports.

When once primary data have been originally collected, moulded by statisticians or statistical machinery, then it becomes secondary in the hands of all other persons who may be desirous of handling it for their own purpose or studies. It follows, therefore, that primary and secondary data are demarcated separately and that the distinction between them is of degree only. If a person 'X' collects some data originally, then the data is primary data to 'X' whereas the same data when used by another person 'Y' becomes secondary data to 'Y'.

## Sources of Secondary Data:

The following are some of the sources of secondary data:

1.  Central and State government publications

2.  Publications brought out by international organisation like the UNO, UNESCO, WHO etc.

3.  Foreign government publications.

4.  Official publications as well as reports of municipalities, zilla parishads etc.

5.  Reports and publications of commissions like UGC, education commission, tariff commission, chambers of commerce, cooperative societies, trade associations, stock exchanges ,banks, business houses etc.

6.  Well known newspapers and journals like the 'Economic Times', 'The Financial Express', 'Indian Journal of Economics', 'Commerce', 'Capital', 'Economical', 'Eastern Economist' etc. Further year books such as Times of India, Yearbook, statesman's Year Book also provided valuable data.

7.  Publications brought out by research institutions, universities as well as those published by the research workers give considerable secondary data.

8.  Through the Internet/ website sources.

Though the above list of secondary data cannot be said to be thorough and complete, yet it can be pointed out that it fairly indicates the chief sources of secondary data. Also, besides the above mentioned data there are a number of other important sources, such as records of governments in various departments, unpublished manuscripts of eminent scholars, research workers, statisticians, economists, private organisations, labour bureaus and records of business firms.

## Verification of secondary data

Before accepting secondary data it is always necessary to scrutinize it properly in regard to its accuracy and reliability. It may perhaps happen that the authorities collecting a particular type of data may unknowingly carry out investigations using procedures wrongly. Hence it is always necessary to carry out the verification of secondary data in the following manner:

i) Whether the organisation that has collected the data is reliable.

ii) Whether the appropriate statistical methods were used by the primary data enumerators and investigators.

iii) Whether the data was collected at the proper time.

iv) Whether the data has timely relevance and is not outdated for present research use by a researcher.

v) Weather the enumerators or compilers of facts and figures had any bias or showed negligence, hurry or carelessness in their compilation work.

vi) Whether the data enumerators had ensured proper standards of accuracy. If so, upto what degree of accuracy.

P.T.O.

## Specimen questionnaire

# Questionnaire

For domestic tourists: part A

For inbound [foreign tourists] part A and part B

## Part A

1.  Name:_____

2.  Address:_____

3.  Sex: Male ☐          Female          ☐

4.  Age:_____

5.  Education: School/SSC

    Undergraduate          ☐

    Graduate          ☐

    Post graduate          ☐

    Technical Degree          ☐

6.  Occupation:  i)  Service: Govt. ☐          Private  ☐

    ii)  Executive          ☐

    iii) Self Employed          ☐

    iv) Professional          ☐

    v)  Teacher / Professor          ☐

    vi) House Wife          ☐

    vii) Student          ☐

    viii) Any Other          ☐

7. Your total monthly income, from all sources like salaries, interest, rent and everyone's income at home

        Below Rs. 50000 ☐

        Rs. 50001 - 100000 ☐

        Rs. 100001 - 150000 ☐

        Above Rs. 150001 ☐

If you are a foreign tourist, state your annual income from all sources (in U.S. $) _____

8. Number of members in the family [including your self]

        Below 15 years ☐

        16 years - 30 years ☐

        31 years -45 years ☐

        46 years - 60 years ☐

        Above 60 years ☐

9. Did you travel during the last three years?

Yes ☐     No ☐     In India ☐     Abroad ☐

If yes, which places did you visit

India

| Place | Month /Year |
|-------|-------------|
|       |             |
|       |             |
|       |             |
|       |             |

Abroad

| Place | Month/Year |
|-------|------------|
|       |            |
|       |            |
|       |            |
|       |            |

10. Where did you stay in India?

    ☐ 5star ☐ 4star ☐ 3star ☐ 2star

    ☐ Motel ☐ Tourist Resort ☐ Friends Place

    ☐ Relatives Place ☐ Any Other

11. What are the modes and class of travel?

    AIR         RAIL         BUS         CAR

    ☐ 1st class ☐ A/c 1st class ☐ Private tourist bus ☐ Private

    ☐ Business ☐ 1st class ☐ Govt tourist bus ☐ Hired

    ☐ Economy ☐ A/c 2nd class

12. Indicate in Rupees how much you spent approximately during the last three years for each tour _____

13. With how many members of your family did you travel? _____

14. Is Leave Travel Allowance provided to you?     Yes          No

15. If you avail of LTA, what is its regularity and quantum?

    Once every          years.  Quantum_____

16. Which of the following ways you prefer to spend your holidays?

    Touring the Temple towns of India            ☐

    At a luxury hotel in a hill station in India  ☐

    Lazing at a posh resort                       ☐

    Trekking the Himalayan trails with no fixed itinery ☐

17. As a tourist what are your experiences?

    Railway facilities are

    Adequate ☐     Inadequate ☐

    Tourism authorities are passive

    True ☐     False ☐

    Condition of roads is

    Satisfactory ☐     unsatisfactory ☐

Cleanliness is lacking in some places of pilgrimage

True ☐          False ☐

Travel agents are quite cooperative

Yes ☐          No ☐

18. Which of the following details of information would be beneficial to a tourist?

Various places of tourist interest ☐

Best places worth their visit ☐

Details regarding comfortable and homely places of accomodation ☐

Details regarding availability of tourist guides ☐

Details regarding best shopping centers ☐

19. As a tourist do you prefer to visit to have:

Yoga and meditation camps

Yes ☐          No ☐

Health clubs/ ayur veda based health care centers

Yes ☐          No ☐

Centre of spiritual discourses

Yes ☐          No ☐

Any other

Yes ☐          No ☐

20. During your tours in India, did you visit or participate in

Wild life sanctuaries

Yes ☐          No ☐

Mountaineering clubs

Yes ☐          No ☐

Water sports

Yes ☐         No ☐

Adventure sports camp

Yes ☐         No ☐

21.   Which of the following facilities would you require to be provided for communication in a hotel?

Fax        ☐

E-mail     ☐

Internet   ☐

22.   Do you want to get the handouts of the various sights of the place in the hotel easily?

Yes        ☐

No         ☐

23.   Which of the following facilities would you expect to have in the hotel?

Library           ☐

Shopping complex  ☐

Movie hall        ☐

Conference hall   ☐

24.   Which of the following facilities are essential in a hotel?

Swimming Pool          ☐

Sauna Bath             ☐

Gymnasium              ☐

Sports Recreation Club ☐

25. Which of the following details should be on the website?

Tariff ☐

Tourist locations ☐

Locations from the Airport ☐

**Part B**

26. What type of food do you prefer in Indian hotels?

Indian ☐

Continental ☐

Chinese ☐

27. Do you need a comprehensive package of lodging and boarding or only lodging during your stay in India?

Lodging and boarding ☐

Only lodging ☐

28. Which of the following facilities would you like the hotel to provide during your stay?

Airline bookings ☐

Railway bookings ☐

Private bus/taxi bookings ☐

29. Do you want a chauffer driven vehicle to assist you?

Yes ☐        No ☐

30. Do you expect the hotel to provide you with a tourist guide to assist you?

Yes ☐        No ☐

31. Do you want the hotel to provide you with an interpreter so that understanding tourist guides would be easier?

Yes ☐        No ☐

32. Do you want your room to be in Indian style or Western style?

Indian ☐        Western ☐

33. Do you want the hotel to provide an expert on Indian culture, tradition, festivals and history?

    Yes ☐          No ☐

34. Do you want the hotel to provide a language tutor to learn a particular Indian language?

    Yes ☐          No ☐

35. What you like the traditional Indian customs during your stay, for a change?

    Yes ☐          No ☐

36. Do you want a hotel to co-ordinate the visits of co-tourists so that you can be in groups for the whole of your stay in that place?

    Yes ☐          No ☐

37. Do you want the hotel to provide bus service to important locations and central place in the city?

    Yes ☐          No ☐

38. Do you find the hotels in India costly?

    Yes ☐          No ☐

39. Do you feel that the services provided are commensurate with the cost?

    Yes ☐          No ☐

40. Do you find the services customer oriented?

    Yes ☐          No ☐

41. Do you come to India only as a tourist or on official work or do you combine both?

    Tourist on holiday        ☐

    Official visit            ☐

    Official cum holiday      ☐

42. Do you want the hotels to provide pamphlets with the Do's and Don'ts that will guide you during your stay in India?

    Yes ☐          No ☐

43. Do you feel the hotels should have medico facilities?

    Essential    ☐

    Preferable    ☐

    Not required    ☐

44. Do you want latest currency exchange rates at the hotel itself?

    Yes    ☐        No    ☐

45. Do you want the hotels in India to advertise on CNN/ BBC?

    Yes    ☐        Not required    ☐

46. Do you want hotels in India to have agents abroad?

    Yes    ☐        No    ☐

47. Do you prefer hotel chains?

    Yes    ☐        No    ☐

48. Do you want the hotels to have their own web site on the Internet?

    Essential    ☐        Preferred    ☐

49. Do you feel the hotels in India should be listed with the the Embassy/ Consulates and recommended the places to stay in India for tourists?

    Essential    ☐

    Preferably    ☐

    Not required    ☐

50. How would you rate the hotels in India in general?

    Very good    ☐

    Good    ☐

    Satisfactory    ☐

## Exercise III

### Questions:

1.    Explain the different types of marketing research?

2.    What is a statistical enquiry? Explain the objectives and scope of statistical enquiry.

3.    Explain the different types of a statistical enquiry.

4.    What is Internet marketing? Explain important features of Internet Marketing.

5.    Explanatory notes on:

   a)    Kinds of statistical units.

   b)    Accuracy and Approximation.

   c)    Statistical errors and classes of errors.

6.    What is primary data? Explain the methods of collecting primary date.

7.    What do you understand by secondary data? State some important sources of secondary data.

8.    Distinguish between primary and secondary data.

9.    What is a questionnaire? Explain the precautions you take in drafting a good questionnaire.

10.    What is the difference between a schedule and a questionnaire? Explain giving a suitable illustration.

11.    State the preliminary steps you would take for planning a statistical enquiry.

12.    a)    Define a statistical unit and mention the usual kinds of units employed in statistical work.

   b)    What are the essential points to be observed while choosing a good unit? Giving appropriate reasons, stating what units can be used for the following cases.

      i.       Production of cotton textiles.

      ii.     Labour employed in an industry.

      iii.    Consumption of electricity.

13.     Prepare a suitable questionnaire for conducting consumer survey for Cadbury's drinking chocolate in Pune city.

14.     Draft an appropriate questionnaire for conducting an inquiry into the problems relating to 'maintenance' faced by members of some co-operative housing societies in Nashik city.

15.     The Glory Shopping Mall authorities are interested in obtaining information about the choices of shoppers visiting the mall. Design a suitable questionnaire for ascertaining the expectations of the shoppers in regard to facilities to shoppers, such as parking, children's recreational area, canteen etc.

16.     A market survey is to be carried out among companies for bulk purchase of "laptop computers" for their sales staff. Design a questionnaire which is to be filled by the purchase manager of the company.

17.     Design a questionnaire to assess the feedback of consumers staying in your hotel for around three nights. Make necessary assumptions and state them at the end of your answer. Briefly explain as to how you will analyze this feedback meeting your objectives.

18.     The manger of a shopping mall desires to know the feedback of shoppers visiting the shopping mall. How should he plan the survey? Prepare a detailed plan for the study along with the questionnaire covering feedback aspects on the facilities, ambience and other details.

# Measurement and Scaling Techniques

Measurement stands for the assignment of numbers to the characteristics of persons, objects or events on the basis of certain principles. The methods of measurement consist of:

(a) Nominal scale (b) Ordinal scale (c) Interval scale and (d) Ratio scale

## NOMINAL SCALE

According to this method, numbers are assigned to objects or persons in the process of counting. The procedure consists of classifying persons, events or objects into a number of mutually exclusive groups on the basis of the presence or absence of a particular characteristic. Nominal measurement is characterized by counting. For instance, the number of women employees in a particular bank In regard to nominal scale, mode is the applicable measure of central tendency.

As an example of nominal scale, we have measurements in the following table

| | WORKERS | |
|---|---|---|
| | SKILLED | UNSKILLED |
| EMPLOYED | 324 | 516 |
| UNEMPLOYED | 110 | 120 |

Thus, nominal scales classify objects in accordance with the qualitative characteristics that cannot be ranked. These include characteristics such as age, religion, sex etc. and the various categories of classification are exhaustive and mutually exclusive. Mathematical operations cannot be carried out on nominal scales, even though frequencies can be calculated.

## ORDINAL SCALE

According to this scale, objects can be ranked by using numerals or suitable letters. These are ranking scales according to which objects can be categorized on the basis of "more than" or "less than". Ordinal scale distinguishes two objects with reference to an attribute qualitatively. This scale has only order and not a unique origin or distance. Median is a measure of dispersion that can be used. The co-relation method based on ranks can be used. The non-parametric procedures in regard to statistical signi ficance are also applicable.

Consumer-oriented marketing research is also based on ordinal data. This is because, a consumer can rank the order of his preferences for a number of brands, or different qualities of goods. However, ordinal scale cannot provide a measure of the extent of qualitative substance that an object possesses. Ordinal scale plays an important role in regard to attitude measurement or psychological scaling.

## INTERVAL SCALE

An interval scale shows equality of differences. Intervals indicate equal quantities of the variable that is measured. The numbers indicated on an interval scale can be added or subtracted but cannot be multiplied or divided. Multiplication and division is not possible as there is no unique origin or zero for the scale. For instance, the centigrade and Fahrenheit temperature scales start with different points of origin. In the centigrade scale the freezing point of water, which is the point of origin is zero whereas for Fahrenheit scale the point of origin is 32. Statistical analysis can be carried out on the basis of interval. For example, measures of central tendency such as mean, median or mode and measures of dispersion such as range, standard deviation are based on this scale. Further, t-test, analysis of variance correlation analysis are related to this scale. Interval scale procedure is a common feature in attitude measurement.

## RATIO SCALE

A ratio scale possesses not only the characteristic properties of the interval scale of measurement but also a natural true or absolute zero scale position or point. The values on this scale can be multiplied or divided. For instance, 12 kilograms is a multiple of 6 kilograms (6 x 2) and 6kilograms is exactly half of 12 kilograms. Zero kilogram on the scale represents total absence of the substance of weight. On account of the properties of identity, rank order, distance or difference in magnitude and unique origin the ratio scale is considered as the most superior measurement scale when compared with the other measures: Nominal scale, ordinal scale and interval scale.

## SCALING TECHNIQUES

The instrument that is used for measurement is called a scale and the process of constructing these scales is called scaling. The techniques that are used for the construction of the scales are called scale construction techniques and these are based on the following approaches:

(a) Concensus (b)Item analysis (c)Arbitrary (d) Cumulative scales and (e) Factor scales.

The two important types of techniques are:

(a) Rating Scales and (b) Attitude scales

## RATING SCALES

Theses scales may be discrete or graphic. A discrete scale rates or describes an object or person into certain categories usually five on a discrete (discontinuous) pattern. For instance, the performance of a student in a test may be rated in the following manner:

Very Good

Very Satisfactory

Satisfactory

Poor

Very poor

This is a descriptive scale. Scale can be in terms of grades using alphabets such as A+, A,B+, B, C or numericals such as 5,4,3,2, 1.
The graphic process shows a continuous scale of evaluation.

The measurer can mark his rate at any point on the continuous straight line graph, shown below:

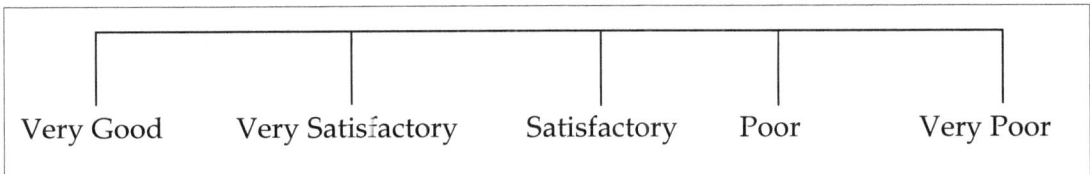

| Very Good | Very Satisfactory | Satisfactory | Poor | Very Poor |

## ATTITUDE SCALES

In modern times, we come across many problems in social sciences and allied areas, where the views, opinions and attitudes of certain groups of persons or individuals play an important role for finding effective solutions to certain social problems .The construction of an attitude scale is based on a certain number of appropriately prepared statements that deal with certain related aspects of the subject matter of the research issue. The respondent gives his appropriate response as to whether he agrees or disagrees with these statements. In accordance with the responses, respondents can be categorized relatively.

The following are some of the well-known types of attitude scales:

1. Thurstone's Differential Scale

2. Likert's Summated Scale

3. Guttman's Cumulative Scale

4. Semantic Differential Scale

## 1    Thurstone's Differential Scale:

An attitude scale based on the technique of equal appearing intervals was devised by L.l Thurstone. This method is based on a large number of statements relating to the views about an idea, practice, an institution or a group of individuals. A panel of judges is approached to study these statements. Each judge is required to place these statements in eleven groups so that the most unfavourable gets placed in the first group and the most favourable in the eleventh group. Statements with which judges do not agree are omitted. Each of these items is assigned a score on the scale, on the basis of the median position of the items assigned by the members of the panel. The final scale that is constructed consists of the relevant number, about20 items.

### Merits

(a)    This scale is useful as a simple and reliable measure in regard to a specific attitude.

(b)    If the judges' views in regard to the classification of the statements have more or less some degree of concurrence, then the scale becomes a consistent instrument.

### Demerits

(a)    For constructing these scales much cost, time and efforts are necessary and this fact is a deterrent for serving as a quick and useful measure.

(b)    The process of dividing the scale into eleven units is quite arbitrary.

(c)    This scale is based on equal-appearing intervals and not with equal intervals and as such, it is not the numerical feature but the psychological aspect that prevails.

(d)    Based on the median score of the scale values of different statements, the same total score pertaining to different persons may not necessarily reflect the same attitudinal approach.

## 2.    Likert's Summated Scale:

Rensis Likert developed the summated rating scale based on item analysis. A particular item is evaluated on the basis of how well it discriminates between those persons whose total score is high and those whose total score is low. A summated scale is based on a series of statements in regard to which an individual expresses his degree of agreement or disagreement through a numerical value on the scale.

The responses may be based on 5-point or 7-point scale. The response to each of the statements is marked in accordance with the degree of agreement or disagreement.

The following is a 5-point scale showing the relevant score values for different degrees of response.

| | Strongly Agree | Agree | Undecided | Disagree | Strongly disagree |
|---|---|---|---|---|---|
| Score | ↓ | ↓ | ↓ | ↓ | ↓ |
| Value | 5 | 4 | 3 | 2 | 1 |

Score value can also be stated as +2   +1   0   -1-2

Likert's scale is of much significance in social science research where the attitudes of individuals play an important role.

The following are the steps for the development of this scale:

(a) A researcher gathers a large number of relevant items pertaining to the attitude under investigation. Each statement points out the favourableness or unfavourableness in regard to the particular attitude. The number of these attitude statements of favourableness and unfavourableness are equal.

(b) The collected statements are administered to a group of individuals. On the basis of a five-point scale these individuals are asked to indicate their responses to the statements.

(c) The 'most favourable' response is given a score 5 and the 'most unfavourable' is given the lowest score 1.

(d) In accordance with the responses of the respondents for all the statements, the total score for each respondent is obtained.

(e)    The investigator may select a significant part (say 25%) of the highest scores and also another significant part (say 25%) of the lowest scores. These two parts represent the 'most favourable' and the 'most unfavourable' attitudes. Thus, the statements that consistently correlate with these two extreme attitudes are finally determined.

(f)    All those statements that consistently correlate are finally selected and retained for the research purpose.

**Merits:**

(a)    For the construction of this, the necessity of a panel of judges does not arise and in this respect it is easier to construct this scale in comparison with the type of scale devised by Thurstone.

(b)    Greater precision and accuracy is ensured in regard to the responses, mainly because the response to each statement is obtained.

(c)    There is not much consumption of time in the construction of the scale.

(d)    There is much scope for the inclusion of some items that may not be directly connected with the attitude under investigation.

(e)    This scale is amenable to usage in the case of investigative studies pertaining to 'respondent centred' and 'stimulus centred'. One can study as to how responses differ under conditions of different stimuli in comparison with responses that ordinarily differ between individuals.

**Demerits**

(a)    The five positions on the Likert's scale are not equally placed. For instance, the interval between 'approve' and 'undecided' may not be equal to that between 'strongly approved' and 'approved'.

(b)    The total score of a respondent can remain the same for different combinations of responses. Hence the total score may not be realistically meaningful.

(c)    There is a possibility that some respondents may answer very much differently from what they honestly feel. This implies that there is a scope for artificiality than for reality. This is an unavoidable limitation of the scale itself.

(d)    The exact degree of responsiveness cannot be precisely expressed. For instance, if a Response deals with 'more agreeable' or 'less agreeable', then the exact extent of agreeability cannot be stated.

## 3. Guttman's Cumumlative Scale

Louis Guttman developed a scaling procedure which is called 'scalogram analysis'. This technique is based on a series of statements that possess a cumulative effect in the sense that the statements which are related amongst themselves form a cumulative series. Accordingly, a respondent who agrees positively to statement No. 5 also agrees positively to statements 4, 3, 2 and 1.This type of scale is characterised by unidimensionality because the responses form a pattern such that an affirmative reply to a statement at one, implies affirmative replies to the statements prior to that end statement .The responses that indicate either agreement or disagreement with the statements are tabulated in the following form which is known as scalogram analysis .

| RESPONDENT CATEGORY | ITEM NO. | | | | | SCORE |
|---|---|---|---|---|---|---|
| | V | VI | III | II | I | |
| A | X | X | X | X | X | 5 |
| B | | X | X | X | X | 4 |
| C | | | X | X | X | 3 |
| D | | | | X | X | 2 |
| E | | | | | X | 1 |
| F | | | | | | 0 |

Hence X denotes agreement with the item

### Interpretation

Here score 3 implies that the respondent is not in agreement with items IV and V but agrees to

Items III, II and l.

## 4. Semantic Differential Scale

This scale refers to a seven point rating procedure in respect of a number of attributes and according to the bipolar adjectives denoting the extreme points. The central position denotes neutrality. The extreme characteristics are given names and the in-between characteristics are represented by blank spaces. The extreme characteristics are of the following type

| Decent | Indecent |
|--------|----------|
| Polite | Impolite |
| Reliable | Unreliable |
| Perfect | Imperfect |
| Pleasant | Unpleasant |

The following is an example relating to customer relationship services of three different hotels, in a certain city, according to a customer survey.

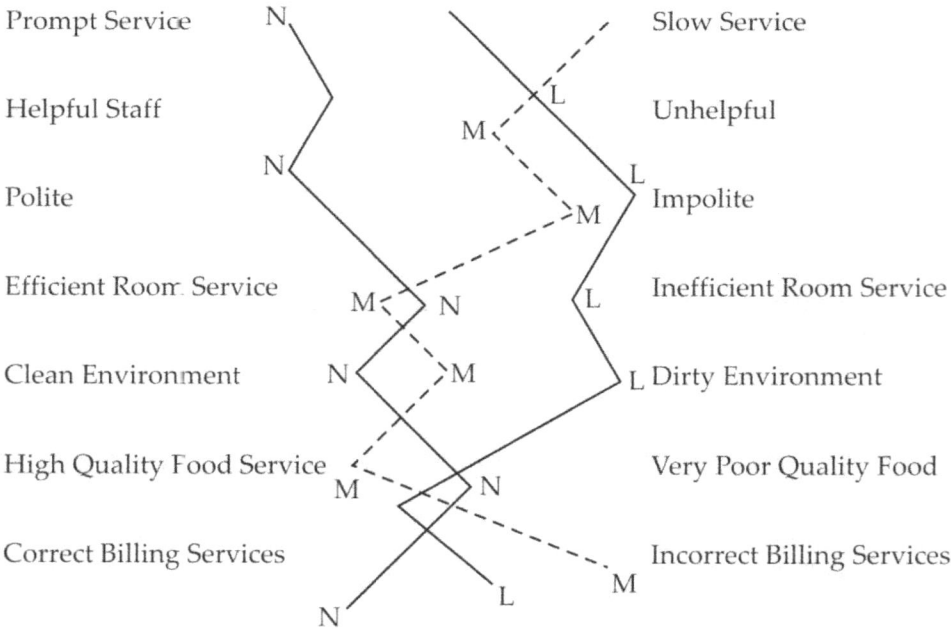

The seven – point rating between the 2 extremes is +3, +2, +1, 0, -1, -2, -3

For the seven attributes maximum scorc is +21 i.e +3x7 and the minimum scroc is -21 i.e -3x7

The scores in respect to the hotels L, M and N are 2 -1 -3 -1 -2 +1 +0 = - 4 for L, and -3 +1 -1 +2 +1 +2 -2 = 0 for M, and 3 +2 +3 +1 +2 -1+2 = 12 for N

On the basis of this scaling for each hotel, the maximum score is 21 and the minimum score is -21. From the score of hotel N it is clear that the food quality service should improve.

## PERFECT MEASUREMENT

Research should always be based on absolutely correct, defect less  and errorless measuring Instruments, tools or procedures of measurement. For this purpose the acceptability of a measuring instrument should be tested on the principles of adherence to the standards of perfect reliability, confirmed practicality and verified validity. The reliability of an instrument can be ensured when it conforms to certain prescribed norms. It is not the physical form or shape but it is the accuracy of the prescribed standard content of the instrument that leads to acceptability. An instrument should be conveniently usable with verifiable validity. Perfection in measurement can be achieved if a researcher, at the outset, carries out appropriately, the prescribed tests of reliability, practical acceptability and validity of his tools of measurement.

## Errors In measurement

Errors in the course of measurement can be traced to a number of factors such as carelessness, negligence, ignorance in the usage of the instrument. If appropriate and defectless instruments are used and care is taken in the process of measurement, only then can accuracy in research be ensured.

In regard to survey-work, where the researcher obtains information through interviews it is necessary, to judge as to whether the respondent is providing accurate facts or is biased. As situational factors also influence measurement, it is imperative that the researcher adopts his measuring procedures accordingly.

Research findings and conclusions can be reliable and acceptable if they are based on sound analysis carried out through appropriate procedures of error-free and perfect measuring tools.

## Evaluation of measurement for perfection.

The following are the three important requirements

I) Validity

II) Reliability

III) Sensitivity

## I) Validity

To ensure accuracy in measurement it is necessary to understand the extent to which a measure can be accepted as valid in terms of accuracy and perfection. For establishing the validity of a measure the following important aspects have to be tested

   i)     Content validity or face validity

   ii)    Criterion validity

   iii)   Convergent validity

   iv)    Discriminant validity

**Content validity:**

Content validity is the subjective aspect. A scale should be representative in the context for the purpose of systematic measurement. It is necessary to ensure that the scale items provide an adequate coverage of the complete domain of the construct that has to be measured. However the content validity is not a totally sufficient measures for ensuring the validity of a scale. No doubt it helps in the explanation of the scale measurements. Content validity can also be considered as face validity.

**Criterion validity:**

Criterion validity aims at examining the performance of a scale in relation to certain variables that are concerned with the attitudinal and behavioural measures of demographic characteristics. In this respect criterion validity can be either concurrent or predictive. Concurrent validity is evaluated on the basis of the development of original instruments which could be administered at the same time to some persons and thereby obtain compatible results. To examine predictive validity an investigator obtains data on the basis of the scale at a certain time and compares it with the data based on criterion variables at a future date.

**Convergent validity:**

Convergent validity is concerned with the degree to which the scale correlates with other measures concerned with the same construct. A researcher has to ensure that conventional scaling techniques are used.

**Discriminate validity:**

When a measure fails to correlate with other constructs then the extent to which this non correlation arises is termed as discriminate validity.

# II) Reliability

Reliability stands for the consistency that is guaranteed in a measure. The reliability of a measuring instrument or a scale can be tested on the basis of the following three methods. Any one of these methods can be considered for reliability acceptance

    a) Test-retest procedure

    b) Cronbach's alpha (coefficient alpha method or split halves method)

    c) Alternative form s method

**a) Test- retest procedure:**

This method is concerned with the assessment of reliability on the basis of repeated tests being conducted by using the same instrument to a group of respondents at two different times when similar or nearly identical situations prevail. The interval between the two times generally varies between 1 to 3 weeks or relevant number of two different dates. The results obtained during the two times are subjected to the finding of correlation coefficient. The positive extent of correlation coefficient indicates the degree of reliability.

**b) Cronbach's alpha( coefficient alpha method or split halves method ):**

According to split half reliability procedure the items concerned with the scales are divided into 2 equal parts and the corresponding scores are examined to access correlation. If there exists a correlation between the two halves then it implies high degree internal consistence. Generally scale items can be split into two halves at random. For this purpose a convenient approach is to use the coefficient alpha or Cronbach's alpha. If the average of all the correlation coefficients relating to all the possible different ways of splitting the scale item is obtained, then it is termed as coefficient alpha which varies from 0 to 1. If Cronbach's alpha is less than or equal to 0.6 then it implies an unsatisfactory internal consistency in respect of reliability. It should be noted that the coefficient alpha tends to increase in its value if the number of scale items increase.

### c) Alternative forms method:

Alternative form's approach for the assessment of reliability necessitates two forms of the scale to be constructed and on the basis of these equivalent forms the same group of respondents are subjected to measurement at two different times.

## III) Sensitivity

The characteristic of sensitivity is applicable to judge the changes in regards to attitudes that are under critical study. The extent to which an instrument is capable of ensuring accuracy is referred to as sensitivity. For instance, in a questionnaire relating to evaluation of performance of banks, a respondents view can be as under to the question:

" considering your own merits and contributions to the bank do you think that you are paid

a) quite well

b) just right

c) too little

d) can't say

Here the respondents sensitivity to provide appropriate answers is very well noticeable.

## EXERCISES IV

**Questions:**

1.      What is measurement? Explain its Importance in research.

2       What is the meaning of 'rating method'? Explain the scales in rating method.

3.      Write explanatory notes on:

(i)     Likert's type scale

(ii)    Scalogram analysis

(iii)   Semantic differential scale

(iv)    Explain the following scales

      (i)     Nominal

      (ii)    Ordinal

      (iii)   Interval

      (iv)    Ratio

6.      Explain the merits and demerits of Thurstone's differential scale.

7.      Explain the uses and limitations Likert's scale

8.      Explain Guttman's cumulative scale

9.      Explain in detail semantic differential scale

10.     State some advantages and limitations of attitude scales

11.     Write explanatory notes on:

(i)     Possible sources of errors in measurement

(ii)    Tests of sound measurement

(iii)   Summated scales

12.     Explain the statement 'Nominal, ordinal and interval scales are statistically non parametric, but ratio scale is parametric'

13.     State whether the following statements are true or false

(i)     Fahrenheit temperature is interval scale

(ii)    Profit and loss, revenue and expenses are on ratio scale.

(iii)   Interval and ratio are normally used with parametric statistics.

(iv)    Nominal and ordinal scales are used with non-parametric statistics.

(v)     When an educationist is asked to rank five business schools then the level of measurement is nominal.

14.   Explain the following statements giving reasons:

(i)     Height, weight and volume are examples relating to ratio scale.

(ii)    Location of origin, i.e., zero is arbitrary in the interval scale.

15.   Discuss the following statements:

(i)     "A measuring instrument should always be judged in terms of convenience, economy and interpretability"

(ii)    "A reliable measuring Instrument contributes to validity"

# Experimentation in Marketing Research

## Meaning of Experimentation

Marketing Research deals with the finding of the causes, bringing about changes in the marketing environment relating to certain products or services. The investigative process that aims at studying the causal relationships between variables by using the control procedures, brings about a situation that is called experimentation .With reference to a marketing problem the experimenter has to manipulate one or more independent variables and keep the others constant. This would enable him to observe the resultant effects. The independent variables are therefore controlled appropriately by the experimenter through manipulation so as to enable himself to observe the changes in the dependent variables.

The designs of experiments are very much necessary in marketing research so as to enable their effective application to the related problems for the purpose of helping managers to make appropriate and correct decisions .The performance of an experiment is based on the understanding of the following terms:

a) Experimental Group

b) Control Group

c) Treatment

d) Replication

e) Extraneous Variation

f) Interactions

g) Confounding

h) Experimental Error

i) Accuracy and Precise Results

## a)   Experimental Group

Experimental group refers to a group of customers or retail stores or malls. The group that is selected is subject to certain treatments whose effects are to be tested, measured and verified .For instance, if two malls located at different places in an area are subjected to certain competitive forces, then it would be interesting to denote one of the two malls as an experimental unit and the second as a control unit. It is desired to find out the extraneous that influence them. In short, it is necessary to determine the nature of external environment. It is supposed that both the malls do attract potential consumers. The sales volumes and as well as the competence of the sales personnel and managerial policies are considered to be more or less similar .Here the experiment is related to the promotions strategy that is introduced at the first mall and the effect of the strategy on the sales is noted by recording the sales during a particular duration of time.

## b)   Control Group

The control group is that group of consumers or malls or concerned market areas to be compared with the experimental group for ascertaining whether the treatments have proved effective. Here the treatment refers to the strategies that are adopted for influencing sales.

## c)      Treatment

Treatment stands for the type of independent variable who's influences and results are being tested by the researcher. For instance, the promotional strategy to increase sales is clearly a treatment. The importance of the treatment has to be judged by the researcher in the course of his experiment.

## d)      Replication

Generally a treatment is adopted for a number of experimental units and such a number of units is called Replication. The more the number of replications, the more appropriate could be the expected response in an experimental group with reference to a certain treatment. It would therefore be necessary on the part of the researchers to consider more replications so as to ensure greater accuracy.

## e)      Extraneous Variation

In spite of researcher's attempts to carry out experiments under controlled situations, still certain variations or changes do arise in experimentation due to conditions (happenings) which cannot be brought within the control of the researcher. If malls are classified in terms of their volume of business, the size of the market's or geographical location, then these factors have an effect on the experimentation based on the treatments. These extraneous variations can also be attributed to the economic environment, government regulations or the nature of the weather at different times.

## f)      Interaction

Interaction stands for the kind of association that may take place between two or more variables. For instance, if we consider two independent variables such as literacy and employment, then the effect of both of these on the living styles can be studied on the basis of the nature of association between literacy and employment.

## g)      Confounding

There are various types of experimental designs which a researcher has to consider while planning an experiment. These experimental designs include

i.      Completely Randomized Design (CRD)

ii.     Randomized Block Design (RBD)

iii.    Latin Square Design or Factorial Design (LSD)

These designs are explained on the basis of certain problems in the following pages.

## h)      Experimental Error

Generally, experiments do bring about certain unavoidable errors as a result of the process of experimentation. These errors measure the variations arise in experimental groups. The variation that is left after eliminating variations caused by extraneous forces. Experimental errors are caused more or less by non application of appropriate standardized techniques in the course of experimentation. Further, there may not be uniformity in the group that is subjected to certain treatments.

## g)      Accuracy and Precise results

Errors do a rise for reasons that are not explainable. However, accuracy is the expected standard which a measurement has to ensure. In short, accuracy and precision respectively refer to standard of measurement and frequency of that standard when measurements are repeated. The different types of errors have been explained in another context in chapter number 3.

## Statistical procedure in experimental designs:

Instead of depending on an opinion survey, a marketer may use the method of experimental design on the basis of his knowledge of the variables and the treatments that can be carried out in regard to a marketing problem. The statistical procedure consist of testing the significance of the variation in treatments. For this purpose the following are the steps:

a)      Problem definition and objectives.

b)      Identification of the variables.

c)      Setting up of Null hypothesis (H0) and also the Alternate hypothesis (H1)

d)      Selection of the appropriate experimental design

e)      Collection of the data and the sample

f)   Analysis and calculations

g)   Interpretation of results

The following problems relating to Marketing Data can be subjected to a randomized design.

## Problem 1

### Completely Randomize design

The data given below shows the prices of five different essential commodities selected from four different shops. Examine whether there is significant difference in the prices of those commodities between the shops.   Use the technique of analysis of variance.

### Treatments

| Shop A | Shop B | Shop C | Shop D |
|--------|--------|--------|--------|
| 11 | 16 | 17 | 18 |
| 14 | 21 | 21 | 8 |
| 13 | 15 | 14 | 16 |
| 12 | 11 | 17 | 10 |
| 15 | 17 | 16 | 13 |

Solution:

**Null hypothesis (H0) :** there is no difference in the average prices of all the essential commodities in the four different shops.

**Alternate hypothesis (H1) :** there is significant difference in the average prices of the essential commodities of the four different shops.

| X1 | $(X1-\overline{X})^2$ | $(X1-\overline{X}1)^2$ | X2 | $(X2-\overline{X})^2$ | $(X2-\overline{X}2)^2$ | X3 | $(X3-\overline{X})^2$ | $(X3-\overline{X}3)^2$ | X4 | $(X4-\overline{X})^2$ | $(X4-\overline{X}4)^2$ |
|---|---|---|---|---|---|---|---|---|---|---|---|
| 11 | 3.06 | 14 | 16 | 1.56 | 0 | 17 | 5.06 | 0 | 18 | 3.06 | 25 |
| 14 | 3.06 | 1 | 21 | 1.56 | 25 | 21 | 5.06 | 16 | 8 | 3.06 | 25 |
| 13 | 3.06 | 0 | 15 | 1.56 | 1 | 14 | 5.06 | 9 | 16 | 3.06 | 9 |
| 12 | 3.06 | 1 | 11 | 1.56 | 25 | 17 | 5.06 | 0 | 10 | 3.06 | 9 |
| 15 | 3.06 | 4 | 17 | 1.56 | 1 | 16 | 5.06 | 1 | 13 | 3.06 | 0 |
| 65 | 15.3 | 10 | 80 | | 52 | 85 | 25.3 | 26 | 65 | 15.3 | 68 |

$$\overline{X}1 = \frac{65}{5} = 13, \quad \overline{X}2 = \frac{80}{5} = 16, \quad \overline{X}3 = \frac{85}{5} = 17, \quad \overline{X}4 = \frac{65}{5} = 13$$

$$\overline{X} = \frac{\overline{X}1 + \overline{X}2 + \overline{X}3 + \overline{X}4}{4} = \frac{13 + 16 + 17 + 13}{4}$$

Between Columns

Sum of squares = 15.3 + 7.8 + 25.3 + 15.3 = 156

Degrees of freedom = 4 – 1 = 3

$$\text{Variance} = \frac{63.70}{3} = 21.23$$

Within Columns

Sum of squares = 10 + 52 + 26 + 68 = 156

Degrees of freedom = No. of items – No of columns = N – C

= 20 – 4 = 16

$$\text{Variance} = \frac{156}{16} = 9.75$$

| ANOVA Table | | | | |
|---|---|---|---|---|
| Source of variation | S.S | d.f. | Variance | F. Ratio |
| Between columns | 63.7 | 3 | 21.23 | $F=\frac{21.23}{9.75}=2.18$ |
| Within columns | 156 | 16 | 9.75 | |
| Total | 219.7 | 19 | | |

Interpretation: The ANOVA table shows the calculated value of F ratio as =2.18 which has to be compared with the table value for d.f. (3.16), F0.05 = 3.24

On comparing the calculated value of F with the table value at 5% level of significance, we find that 2.18 < 3.24. Therefore, there is no significant difference in the prices between the shops. Hence we accept the Null hypothesis (H0) and reject the alternate hypothesis (H1). Therefore, the prices are not influenced by the shops.

## Problem 2

### Randomized block design

Four different Brands of tyres L, M, N, P were tested for their durability. A sample of five tyres of each brand was tested on the basis of thousands of kilometers covered before total wear out. With reference to the data given below, carry out analysis of variance to examine whether there is significant difference between the brands.

| L | M | N | P |
|---|---|---|---|
| 32 | 39 | 43 | 37 |
| 45 | 41 | 37 | 34 |
| 38 | 44 | 29 | 29 |
| 35 | 36 | 31 | 33 |
| 40 | 30 | 40 | 27 |

**Solution:**

H0 : there is no difference in regard to the durability between the brands.

H1 : there is significant difference in the Brands in regard to their durability.

After carrying out the necessary calculations, we find the ANOVA table as under:

ANOVA Table

| Source of variation | S,S | d.f | var | F. Ratio | F 0.05=3.24 for d.f (3,16) |
|---|---|---|---|---|---|
| Between Brands | 120 | 3 | 40 | 40/26=1.538 | 1.538<3.24 Not significant |
| Within Brands | 416 | 16 | 26 | | |

On comparison between the calculated value of F and the table value, we find that there is no significant difference (1.538 < 3.24). Hence, H0 is accepted and H1 is rejected.

## Randomized block design

Here the procedure involves the grouping of the different units into homogeneous groups or blocks (for replication). The purpose of grouping is to reduce the experimental error to the extent possible. The problem explained below would clarify the working.

The following problem:

The data given below shows the yields of four different varieties of wheat from four different (agricultural) Blocks.

| Blocks / Varieties | B1 | B2 | B3 | B4 |
|---|---|---|---|---|
| V1 | 17 | 28 | 26 | 32 |
| V2 | 24 | 23 | 28 | 30 |
| V3 | 31 | 19 | 21 | 39 |
| V4 | 40 | 25 | 30 | 40 |

**Solution:** Subtracting 30 from each one of the values of the data we get

| Blocks / Varieties | B1 | B2 | B3 | B4 | Total |
|---|---|---|---|---|---|
| V1 | -13 | -2 | -4 | 2 | -17 |
| V2 | -6 | -7 | -2 | 0 | -15 |
| V3 | 1 | -11 | -9 | 9 | -10 |
| V4 | 10 | -5 | 0 | 10 | 15 |
| V5 | -8 | -25 | -15 | 21 | -27 |

According to the shortcut method, we calculate the correction factor as equal to the quotient obtained on dividing the square of the total of the given values by the number of values

That is

$$CF = \frac{T^2}{N}$$

Here

$$CF = \frac{(-27)^2}{16} = 45.56$$

Variances between columns

$$S.S = [\frac{(-8)^2}{4} + \frac{(-25)^2}{4} + \frac{(-15)^2}{4} + \frac{(21)^2}{4}] - CF$$

$$= [\frac{64 + 625 + 225 + 441}{4}] - 45.56$$

$$= 293.19$$

$$d.f. = C - 1$$

$$= 4 - 1 = 3$$

$$Variance = \frac{293}{3} = 97.73$$

Variances between rows

$$S.S = [\frac{(17)^2}{4} + \frac{(-15)^2}{4} + \frac{(-10)^2}{4} + \frac{(15)^2}{4}] - CF$$

$$=[\frac{289+225+100+225}{4}]-45.56$$

$$=164.19$$

$$d.f. = r - 1$$

$$= 4 - 1$$

$$= 3$$

$$Variance = \frac{164.19}{3} = 54.73$$

Total sum of squares

S.S=$[(13)^2 + (-6)^2 + 1+(10)^2 + (-2)^2 + (-7)^2 + (-11)^2 +(-5)^2 +(-4)^2 +(-2)^2 +(-9)^2 +0 +(2)^2+0 +(9)^2+(10)^2 ] - CF$

$$=[169+36+1+100+4+49+121+25+16+4+81+4+81+100] -CF$$

$$=791 - 45.56$$

$$=745.44$$

Degrees of Freedom  =cr – 1

$$=4x4 - 1$$

$$=15$$

## ANOVA Table

| Source of variation | S.S | d.f | Variance | F Ratio | Table value of F at 5% level |
|---|---|---|---|---|---|
| Between columns (blocks) | 293.19 | 3 | 97.73 | $\frac{97.73}{32.01}=3.05$ | F=3.86 d.f.(3,9) |
| Between rows(varieties) | 164.19 | 3 | 54.73 | $\frac{54.73}{32.01}=1.71$ | F=3.86 d.f.(3,9) |
| Residual | 288.06 | 9 | 32.01 | | |
| Total | 745.44 | 15 | | | |

On comparing the calculated values of F with the corresponding table values of F we find that 3.05<3.86 and 1.71<3.86

Therefore there is no significant difference due to varieties or due to blocks.

## Problem 3:

**Latin Square Design (LSD):**
The data given below shows the monthly sales of 4 salesmen in 4 different cities .

Months

|  | M1 | M2 | M3 | M4 |
|---|---|---|---|---|
| C1 | 32 | 56 | 46 | 54 |
| C2 | 42 | 39 | 50 | 29 |
| C3 | 63 | 38 | 40 | 41 |
| C4 | 40 | 42 | 55 | 33 |

Carry out the analysis on the basis of experimental combinations (LSD)

**Solution:**
The above given data has been rearranged on the basis of the sales, of the salesmen.

S1 S2 S3 S4 in the cities C1 C2 C3 C4 in the respective cities.

|  | S1 | S2 | S3 | S4 |
|---|---|---|---|---|
| C1 | 32 | 29 | 56 | 33 |
| C2 | 46 | 39 | 63 | 42 |
| C3 | 54 | 42 | 41 | 55 |
| C4 | 38 | 50 | 40 | 40 |

This data is simplified on the basis of coding method. 50 has been deducted from each of the above figures and we get the table.

|  | S1 | S2 | S3 | S4 | Total |
|---|---|---|---|---|---|
| C1 | -18 | -21 | 6 | -17 | -50 |
| C2 | -4 | -11 | 13 | -8 | -10 |
| C3 | 4 | -8 | -9 | 5 | -8 |
| C4 | -12 | 0 | -10 | -10 | -32 |
| Total | -30 | -40 | 0 | -30 | -100 |

The correction factor is $(c.f) = \dfrac{T^2}{N} = \dfrac{(-100)^2}{16} = 625$

After further simplification we get the following ANOVA table

### ANOVA table

| Source of variation | d.f | S.S | Var. | F ratio | Table Value |
|---|---|---|---|---|---|
| Between treatments | 3 | 225 | 225/3 = 75 | 75/227.5=0.329 | 3.29 |
| Between Rows | 3 | 297 | 297/3 = 99 | 99/227.5 = 0.435 | 3.29 |
| Between columns | 3 | 146 | 146/3 = 48.67 | 48.67 / 227.5 = 0.213 | 3.29 |
| Error | 6 | 1365 | 1365 / 6 = 227.5 | | |
| Total | 15 | | | | |

I. Hypothesis Treatment (salesmen)

$H_0$ : S1 = S2 = S3 = S4 (Treatments Means are equal)

$H_1$ : Treatments Means are not equal.

II. Hypothesis for cities (rows)

$H_0$ : C1 = C2 = C3 = C4 (Rows Means are equal)

$H_1$ : Row Means are not equal.

III. Hypothesis for months (columns)

$H_0$ : H1 = H2 = H3 = H4 (Columns Means are equal)

$H_1$ : Columns Means are not equal.

Simplification in respect of Experimental Combinations provided the following LSD:

|  | M1 | M2 | M3 | M4 | Total |
|---|---|---|---|---|---|
| C1 | -18 | 6 | 4 | 4 | -12 |
| C2 | -8 | -11 | 0 | -21 | -40 |
| C3 | 13 | -12 | -10 | -9 | -18 |
| C4 | -10 | -8 | 5 | -17 | -30 |
| Total | -23 | -25 | -9 | -43 | -100 |

Variance between columns

$$SS = \left[ \frac{(-23)^2}{4} + \frac{(-25)^2}{4} + \frac{(-9)^2}{4} + \frac{(-43)^2}{4} \right] - CF$$

$$= \left[ \frac{529}{4} + \frac{625}{4} + \frac{81}{4} + \frac{1849}{4} \right] - 625$$

$$= \left[ \frac{3084}{4} \right] - 625$$

$$= 771 - 625$$

$$= 146$$

Total sum of squares (TSS)

$=[(-18)^2 +(-8)^2+ (13)^2 + (-10)^2 + (6)^2 + (-11)^2 + (-12)^2 + (-8)^2 + (-4)^2 + (0) + (-10)^2 + (5)^2 + (4)^2 + (-21)^2 + (-9)^2 + (-17)^2] - C.F.$

$= [324 + 64 + 169 + 100 + 36 + 121 + 144 + 64 + 16 + 0 + 100 + 25 + 16 +441 +81 +289]- 625$

$= 1990 - 625$

$=1365$

## Interpretation :-

1. **Testing Hypothesis I**

   On comparing the calculated value with the table value we find that 0.329 < 3.29. Therefore, the ratio is not significant . Therefore $H_0$ is accepted. Therefore the Treatment Means are equal. Therefore the abilities of the salesmen are more or less the same.

2. **Testing Hypothesis II**

   On comparing the calculated value with the table value we find that 0.435 < 3.29. Therefore, the F ratio is not significant . Therefore $H_0$ is accepted. Therefore the sales figures corresponding to the 4 cities are more or less the same.

3. **Testing of Hypothesis III**

   On comparing the calculated value with the table value we find that 0.213 < 3.29. Therefore, the ratio is not significant . Therefore $H_0$ is accepted. Therefore the average sales figures for the 4 months are more or less the same.

## Exercise V

### Questions:

1.  Four different brands of motor car tyres were tested for their durability. These tyres belong to 4 different tyre manufacturing companies. Example of 5 tyres of each brand was tested on the basis of 1000's of kilometres covered before total wear out. Carry out analysis of variance and interpret the results relating to the data given below

    | A | B | C | D |
    |----|----|----|----|
    | 23 | 38 | 44 | 39 |
    | 54 | 40 | 38 | 36 |
    | 83 | 43 | 30 | 31 |
    | 53 | 35 | 32 | 35 |
    | 42 | 34 | 50 | 29 |

2.  The following data shows the prices of 4 essential articles in 5 different shops. Carry out an analysis of variance.

    |    | A | B | C | D |
    |----|----|----|----|----|
    | S1 | 12 | 17 | 9 | 7 |
    | S2 | 8 | 11 | 18 | 16 |
    | S3 | 14 | 9 | 12 | 18 |
    | S4 | 16 | 23 | 21 | 25 |
    | S5 | 10 | 10 | 20 | 24 |

3.  The data given below shows the number of refrigerators sold by 4 salesmen during 4 different months. Carry out an analysis of variance.

    | | Salesmen | | | |
    |-------|----|----|----|----|
    | month | S1 | S2 | S3 | S4 |
    | M1 | 32 | 29 | 56 | 33 |
    | M2 | 46 | 39 | 63 | 42 |
    | M3 | 54 | 42 | 41 | 55 |
    | M4 | 38 | 50 | 40 | 40 |

4.    The following data shows the number of units of a product manufactured by 4 different workers using 3 different machines

| Machines | | | |
|---|---|---|---|
| Workers | M1 | M2 | M3 |
| W1 | 23 | 42 | 31 |
| W2 | 36 | 56 | 29 |
| W3 | 21 | 34 | 50 |
| W4 | 30 | 28 | 40 |

Do you find the same mean productivity for the 3 machines?

Do the 4 workers differ with respect to the mean productivity?

5.    With reference to the data given below, carry out an analysis of variance.

| Salesmen | | | | |
|---|---|---|---|---|
| City | A | B | C | D |
| C1 | 23 | 17 | 24 | 26 |
| C2 | 47 | 44 | 28 | 36 |
| C3 | 30 | 29 | 18 | 48 |

6.    Carry out an analysis of variance relating to the yield of 4 different varieties of a crop in 4 different blocks

| Blocks | | | | |
|---|---|---|---|---|
| Varieties | B1 | B2 | B3 | B4 |
| V1 | 27 | 26 | 30 | 25 |
| V2 | 22 | 20 | 24 | 20 |
| V3 | 19 | 18 | 22 | 21 |
| V4 | 24 | 25 | 28 | 23 |

7.    What is experimentation? Explain the relevant terms relating to the performance of an experiment.

8.    Describe briefly the statistical procedure that should be adopted with reference to an experimental design.

9.      Write an explanatory note on the statistical procedure for testing the significance of variation in treatments.

10.     With reference to marketing data describe the statistical procedure to be followed with respect to the following designs:
        i)      CRD
        ii)     Randomised block design
        iii)    Latin square design

# Sampling Techniques

The word 'sample' means a part of any collection of things, individuals or results of operations that are quantitatively expressed. A totality or a collection of things or individuals is said to constitute a population. Hence a sample simply means a part of a population. A finite population is one that has individuals or things that can be finitely expressed in numerical terms, whereas an infinite population is one that cannot be expressed finitely. For example, the heights of 100 persons form a finite population whereas all the heavenly bodies such as stars are infinite. Population is also called universe. The following are a few examples of finite populations: population of marks of students at an examination, population of prices, weights, incomes etc.

To draw certain conclusions about the characteristics of a population it is sufficient to select and study a part of it. In short, for the purpose of statistical studies, a sample would suffice. The entire work of selecting samples from a population is termed sampling.

## MAIN OBJECT OF SAMPLING

The principle aim of selecting a sample and studying it is to acquire the maximum information about the population with the least amount of time, money and energy. In brief, maximum information with minimum effort is the goal of sampling.

## BASIC PRINCIPLES OF SAMPLING

Before undertaking the work of sampling it is necessary to bear in mind the following

**points:**

1.  No bias or prejudice should creep into the selection of a sample or samples.

2.  All the members of the sample should be governed by the same rules and conditions of sampling.

3.  Individual members of the sample should be entirely independent of one another.

4.  Special importance should never be attached to certain parts of the population while selecting members for the sample.

### Importance of Sampling Methodology in marketing research

Sampling is very much used in marketing research because it helps the marketing manager in the process of decision making. Managers realize the merits of the different samples and their respective sizes so as to minimize the errors that maybe inherent in them. The qualities of sampling consist of adaptability, economy, speed and the scientific procedure.

Amongst the methods of sampling there are two categories: probability sampling and non- probability sampling. In probability sampling, the process of selecting members is based on the chance factor. If the process of selection is not based on chance but on some arbitrary method. then it is non-probability sampling.

## Methods of Probability Sampling

The following methods of sampling deserve special study:

1. Random Sampling.

2. Systematic Sampling.

3. Cluster Sampling.

4. Area Sampling.

5. Stratified Sampling.

6. Multistage Sampling.

1. **Simple Random Sampling:** A sample that consists of members that are chosen at random from a population is called a random sample; the entire process of selecting members at random from a population is known as random sampling. This method ensures that the probability of each member of the population in the sample is equal. In other words, each member has the same chance of being included in the sample. Random sampling is a good method mainly because members of the sample are chosen not only without bias or prejudice but purely according to the principles of random sampling. Further, to overcome bias or errors due to human weakness, certain methods of random sampling have been devised. For instance, the following are some of the methods:

(a)     Method based on mechanical devices,

(b)     Method based on random sampling numbers.

One of the simplest devices is the lottery drum method. Here, members of the population are numbered on tickets of uniform size and colour. These tickets are placed in a drum. Just like a pure lottery, tickets are drawn at random. In the case of a small size random sample, a simple device is to number all members of the population on small identical Cards of a uniform size and colour, like playing cards and draw them from the pack, one by one, with replacement after each shuffle  and drawing. This procedure is continued till the cards drawn give the required size of the random sample.

In the case of large scale random sampling, these methods are not considered to be useful. Hence tables of random sampling numbers such as Tippets random sampling numbers or Kendall and Babington-Smith's random sampling numbers are used.

2.  **Systematic Sampling:** When complete population lists are available, this method of sampling is considered to be the most appropriate one. Further. it is a quick and easy method. The method consists of selecting at random the first member and thereafter the other members in a systematic way. For example, if a population list comprises 48,000 members and a sample of 800 is required, then we can select every sixtieth item of the population. But before doing that it is necessary to select the first member by random sampling, from the numbers 1 to 60. For instance if 22 happens to be the number selected at random then it will be the first number, 82 will be the second number, 142 the third and so on.

    Being quick and simple, this method of sampling is considered to be very useful and hence it has universal application.

3.  **Cluster Sampling:** This method of sampling is based on groups of units or clusters of units or observations. Each cluster is generally homogenous. From each cluster members are selected at random. In this manner the different clusters are represented. Further, from a universe or population of clusters some clusters may be selected on the basis of random sampling. In other words, the representation by clusters on random sampling basis simplifies the task of the researcher.

4.  **Area Sampling:** A universe may consist of a totality of various areas (geographically) or blocks consisting of certain towns or cities. When random sampling is applied for selecting some areas from a universe of areas, then such a method represents the universe in a representative manner.

5.  **Stratified Sampling:** The word stratification simply means division into strata or separate groups. In the singular, a group is called a stratum. A population is usually far from homogeneous; it is to a marked extent heterogeneous. When a population is divided into a certain number of strata then the number of members to be selected from a particular stratum by random sampling is proportional to the size of the stratum. All individual items selected by random sampling from each stratum constitute a sample called the stratified sample. Therefore, the process of such a sample selection is termed stratified sampling. When compared

with the systematic and random sampling methods, stratified sampling prominently stands out as the better choice. This is because it overcomes the chief hurdle of random sampling, viz, giving unequal representation. Here unequal representation implies that certain parts of the population may be better represented than others in the sample. Further, the random sampling technique introduces a certain element of unequal representative ness in the selection of members which is not so in the ease of stratified sampling. The chief merit of this method, apart from stratification, is that the manner of picking up items from each stratum is purely according to random sampling principles.

6. **Multistage Sampling:** This is the best method to use when large scale nationwide Surveys are to be undertaken. The notable fact about this method is that the entire sampling is undertaken in a certain number of stages depending upon the nature of the survey. The only problem is that larger the number of stages, the greater is the likelihood of accuracy being sacrificed.

The chief merit of this method of sampling is that it is less expensive and more practicable. Here's an example of how multistage sampling draws random samples at each of the different stages. For a study of the smoking habits of people inhabiting a particular State, a multistage sampling maybe undertaken as follows: the process of selecting a few districts in the State by random sampling constitutes the first stage; selecting by random sampling a few towns and cities from these selected districts constitutes the second stage; selecting by random sampling a few blocks and localities from these selected towns and cities constitutes the third. Finally, selecting by random sampling, individuals from these selected blocks and localities constitutes the final stage.

## Methods of Non- Probability Sampling:

1. Purposive Sampling
2. Judgement Sampling
3. Convenience Sampling
4. Quota Sampling

1. **Purpose Sampling:** The main object of this technique is to serve a particular purpose. Members of the sample are chosen strictly according

to the criterion laid down. This sampling is also known as judgement sampling. As the individual members of the sample are chosen in accordance with a certain principle, the method of such a selection is called purposive sampling. The nature of this sampling technique is such that members of the population have unequal probabilities of inclusion in the sample, which in turn means that some members have a very high probability of inclusion over others. For instance, while undertaking an opinion survey, only the personal judgement of a particular group of persons may be taken into consideration. This is mainly due to the purposive nature of the survey.

2. **Judgment Sampling:** According to this method, a market researcher basically is concerned in obtaining appropriate information in regard to the consumers preferences and the reasons for such preferences. Further, in accordance with the nature of the product he has to decide as to which segment would be appropriate for his research. Having judged that, he has to select some units based on his judgment. Judgment serves the purpose of understanding the exact representativeness of the units that are being selected. Hence, judgment is of much relevance in marketing research.

3. **Convenience Sampling:** It is quite obvious that a researcher can independently on the basis of his own choice select some of those units of the universe without any pre-judgment. In short, it is convenience that matters most. This type of sampling is also of much relevance when units are required to be selected purely to suit the convenience of the researcher.

4. **Quota Sampling:** Depending upon the nature of marketing research, a researcher may select from a given population a certain part of that population in accordance with a prescribed quota (prescribed number of units). The quota is considered to be adequate and representative of the concerned population.

## STATISTICAL LAWS

We now consider the following basic laws which provide the background to sampling techniques:

1. The Law of Statistical Regularity.
2. The Law of Inertia of Large Numbers.

1. **The law of Statistical Regularity:** This law asserts that a sample will always show the characteristics of the population to which it belongs. In other words, when a few members from a population are chosen at random, then the members so selected undoubtedly explain the nature of the population. Further, whatever be the selected part of the population, it will reflect to a certain extent the regular characteristics of the entire population. In short, the philosophy of this law is that a part represents the whole.

Let us take an example, if we consider the marks secured by 40 candidates in a subject, amongst 200 candidates, then clearly the arithmetic average of the marks of these 40 candidates will not differ much from the average of the marks of all the 200 candidates. Of course, we might observe that the larger the sample size, the more negligible would be the difference. The utility of this law can be at once seen when we deal with statistics of life insurance. Even statistics of agricultural experiments indicate the significance of this law.

2. **The law of Inertia of Large Numbers:** This law simply means that larger the sample size, the stronger would be its position in fully representing the entire population. In other words, large samples always tend to give more accurate results about the population to which they belong. For example, if we toss a coin only a few times then the proportion of tails to the total number of tosses is likely to differ significantly from the proportion of the number of heads to the total number of tosses. But if we toss a coin a large number of times then there is every possibility for the proportions of heads and tails to be each equal to 1/2. This clearly points out that large samples are always more stable, in the sense that they represent the population more accurately.

## Errors in Sampling

In the course of the sampling procedure the following two kinds of errors may araise:

1) Sampling errors
2) Non Sampling errors

1) **Sampling errors:** When samples are selected on the basis of an estimated sample size, an error may arise due to want of accuracy in the representative characteristic of the sample. It is apparent that when different samples of the same size are selected from a given population and the respective arithmetic means of the samples are calculated, then it can be easily determined that the arithmetic mean of all these means will be exactly equal to the mean of the population. In other words, the mean of the sampling distribution is equal to the mean of the population. But the mean of the standard deviations of all the samples is not equal to the standard deviation of the population. This is a statistical error. Here the standard deviation of the sampling distribution is called a standard error. A statistical error can be reduced by taking a larger sample from a given population.

2) **Non-Sampling errors:** Non-sampling errors may arise due to unintentional mistakes in the collection, enumeration or recording of data. Also they may arise due to faulty measurements. Further, intentional errors are deliberate errors that are also called biased errors.

## a.    Sample Size

The mean of a given population can also be estimated from a sample mean of the sample size as explained below. The sample size is based on 3 different specifications.

a)    The specification of error (e). This error is based on the permissibility in the estimate.

b)    The degree of confidence that can be reposed in the estimated sample size (95% or 99% as the case may be)

c)    The estimate of the standard deviation of the universe relating to the marketing study.

The following problems explain the procedures.

## Problem 1 :

Find the sample size N given that

e = 0.9

$\sigma$= 12.4 and

Z = 1.96 at 95% level of confidence

**Solution:**

$$n=\frac{z^2\sigma^2}{e^2}$$

$$=\frac{(1.96)^2 (12.4)^2}{(0.9)^2}$$

=729.2

=729.0 approximately

## Problem 2:

In the case of an estimate that is qualitative, the proportional characteristics are used. The formula is

n = Z² PQ

   e²

where:

e = estimated error

P = proportion of characteristic

Q = 1- P    and

Z = corresponds to 1.96 at 5% level of significance

Given,

e = 0.20

Z = 1.96

P = 0.12

Q = 0.88

$$n = \frac{(1.96)^2 (0.12)(0.88)}{(0.20)^2}$$

$$n = \frac{0.40567296}{0.04}$$

n = 10.1418

## b. Sample size

For the calculation of sample size the following formula can also be used.

Sample size $\quad n = \dfrac{N}{1 + Ne^2} \quad$ (Given by Toro Yemane)

where $\qquad$ N = total population

$\qquad$ e = error (confidence level) such as 5% or 10% that is 0.05 or 0.10

## Problem 1:

Suppose $\quad$ N = 10000

$\qquad$ e = 0.05, then

$$n = \frac{10000}{1 + 10000(0.05)^2} = \frac{10000}{1 + 25}$$

$$= 384.615$$

$$= 385 \text{ approximately}$$

A random sample of size 385 would represent a population of 10000 at 5% level (error)

## Problem 2:

Suppose  $N = 60000$ and e = 0.10

then,   $$\frac{6000}{1 + 6000(0.10)^2} = 98.36$$

= 98 approximately

Sample size in the case of proportions

$$n = (\frac{Z}{e})^2 \ pq \qquad \text{(Given by Fink and Kosecoff)}$$

where,

$Z$ = standard limit depending upon confidence level. For instance, 1.96 limit corresponds to 5 % level.

e = sampling error such as 0.05

p = the given proportion.

## Problem 3:

Suppose   z = 1.96

$$e = 0.05$$

$$p = 0.20$$

then,  $n = (\frac{Z}{e})^2 pq$

$$= (\frac{1.96}{0.05})^2 (0.20)(0.80)$$

$$= 245.8624$$

$$= 246 \text{ approximately}$$

Method of deriving the formula for finding the sample size

We know that the sampling error $\bar{x} - \mu$, $\bar{x}$ = sample mean, $\mu$ = population mean.

Confidence limits for m are $\bar{x} \pm Z(SE)$ where Z is the confidence coefficient such as 1.96 at 5% level of significance and SE is the standard error.

$$\bar{x} - \mu = Z(SE)$$

$$e = Z\,(SE) = Z\left(\frac{\sigma}{e}\right)$$

$$e = Z\left(\frac{\sigma}{\sqrt{n}}\right) \quad \text{i.e.} \quad \sqrt{n} = Z\frac{\sigma}{\sqrt{e}}$$

$$n = Z^2\frac{\sigma}{e^2} = \left(\frac{Z}{e}\right)^2 \sigma^2$$

$\sigma$ = Standard deviation of the population

In regard to proportions

$$n = \left(\frac{Z}{e}\right)^2 pq \quad \text{i.e.} \quad n = = \left(\frac{Z}{e}\right)^2 p\,(1-p)$$

(vi) Use of tables for finding the sample size

A researcher can use the tables prepared by Eckhardt, on the basis of the values of p, E and Z, E is the error and Z is the confidence level. Refer Echardt (Social Research Methods, 1978 : 400)

(vii) Problems with reference to stratified sampling and cluster sampling

## Problem 4:

According to a survey on the basis of income levels, a researcher divides 25000 families into five strata as mentioned below:

Stratum 1: Income less than Rs. 5000 p.m = 8000

Stratum 2: Income less than Rs. 15000 and above Rs. 5000 = 10000

Stratum 3: Income less than Rs. 50000 p.m = 4000

Stratum 4: Income less than Rs. 1 lakh p.m = 2500

Stratum 5: Income above Rs. 1 lakh p.m = 500

Suppose the researcher has to study an appropriately representative sample of 100 families, then according to proportional method, he has to select at random from each stratum, the number of members mentioned below, as per the calculations:

Stratum 1: Sample size $= \dfrac{8000}{25000} \times 100 = 32$

Stratum 2: Sample size $= \dfrac{10000}{25000} \times 100 = 40$

Stratum 3: Sample size $= \dfrac{4000}{25000} \times 100 = 16$

Stratum 4: Sample size $= \dfrac{2500}{25000} \times 100 = 10$

Stratum 5: Sample size $= \dfrac{500}{25000} \times 100 = 2$

The final sample size $= 32 - 40 + 16 + 10 + 2 = 100$

## Strata with Different Variability

We consider strata that not only differ in their sizes but also in their respective variability. Therefore, in regard to variability within a stratum, the standard deviation has to be taken into account.

Suppose we consider as the number strata

i.e.        $N_1, N_2, N_3, \ldots N_x$ with standard deviations

$S_1, S_2, S_3, \ldots S_x$ = respectively and

$n = n_1 + n_2 + \ldots n_x$ where $n_1, n_2, n_3, \ldots n_x$ denote the respective sample sizes of the x strata then the sample size of the $p^{th}$ strata is given by

$$n_p = \dfrac{n.N_p S_p}{N_1 S_1 + N_2 S_2 + \ldots + N_x S_x}$$

where        $p = 1, 2, 3 \ldots x$

## EXERCISE VI

### Question:

1.   Discuss the methods generally used in sampling. Explain in brief the law of statistical regularity.

2.   Distinguish between population and sample. What do you understand by a random sample and how is it drawn?

3.   What is sampling? What are the requisites of a good sample? Describe any two methods of sampling.

4.   What is a random sample? Discuss the merits and demerits of census and sample surveys.

5.   What is meant by sample method of enquiry? When is it adopted? What are its advantages? What are the essential requisites of a good sample?

6.   Explain the terms 'sample' and 'population'. Distinguish between census and sample survey.

7.   Describe briefly the stratified and systematic sampling methods.

8.   Explain the methods of systematic and stratified sampling with suitable illustrations.

9.   State the merits claimed by the method of random sampling in statistical surveys.

10.   Compare and contrast the merits and demerits of the sample survey and census methods:

11.   Write short notes on:

  (i)    Random sampling
  (ii)   Systematic sampling
  (iii)  Purposive sampling
  (iv)   Stratified sampling
  (v)    Multistage sampling

(vi)    Law of statistical regularity

(vii)   Law of inertia of large numbers

12.   Describe any two sampling methods with suitable illustrations.

13.   What is sampling? What are the requisites of a good sample?

14.   Explain what is meant by chance sampling and systematic sampling. Give illustrations of situations in which they are appropriate. State the laws of statistical regularity and explain how they are the basis of inference drawn from samples.

15.   Write notes on:

(i)    Statistical populations and samples

(ii)   Stratified sampling

16.   Describe briefly the following:

(i)    Simple random sampling

(ii)   Stratified random sampling.

(iii)  Systematic sampling

17.   Define the meaning of random sampling', and explain why the randomness is important in sample design. Explain with illustrations how the use of stratification affects randomness of a sample.

18.   Describe briefly probability methods of sampling and non-probability methods of sampling.

19.   What is sampling design? Give sampling design in the following case to assess average household expenditure on food and entertainment by different cross sections of Indian population .

20.   With the increasing disposable income the lifestyle of the urban youths is changing. They require different places to 'hang out' and socialize. This has helped the multiplex industry. This industry not only offers movies, but host of food courts, gaming zones. A multi national chain of multiplex is planning to enter and start a multiplex in your city. It has entrusted you with carrying out a research to find out customer's expectations from multiplex.

      a.       Prepare a research proposal to be submitted to the organization

      b.       What sampling techniques would be appropriate for this project.

21.    Draft a research proposal for following case:

A customer satisfaction study is to be carried out for Indian railways for their passenger travelling between Pune and Delhi. Also describe the process of selecting sample in this case. How will you calculate sample size in this case.

# Testing of hypothesis (I) Large and small samples

The basic purpose in selecting a sample from a given population is to find out how far the sample effectively represents the population. Measures relating to certain characteristics of a population are known as parameters while those relating to a sample are called "statistics". The unknown parameters of a population are estimated through sample statistics and this is the process of estimation. Further, we make certain suppositions known as hypothesis about population parameters; these hypotheses are our expectations. We test by finding out the difference between our observations of some statistics of a sample with the corresponding parameters of the population. This process of testing is known as the significance of statistical hypothesis. As a sample is a part of a population, there will be some difference between the value of the estimate derived from a sample and the supposed parametric value of the population. This is known as sampling error.

Suppose from a population of size N, we draw sample of size n, then the number of such samples that can be drawn would be NCn (Combinations). Suppose we calculate the means of all the samples, then we will have NCn means. The frequency distribution representing these means is called sampling distribution.

It can now be observed that the mean of the sampling distribution is always equal to the mean of the respective population. But the standard deviation of the sampling distribution is not equal to the standard deviation of the population. The standard deviation of the sampling distribution is called the 'standard error'. It is denoted by S.E. and is equal to $\dfrac{\sigma}{\sqrt{n}}$ where $\sigma$ is the S.D and n is the sample size.

It should be noted that a sampling distribution is generated from a population and the same population may give rise to an infinite number of sampling distributions of the concerned statistics.

## Hypothesis and level of significance

In setting up a hypothesis, we begin with a 'null hypothesis' which states that there is no difference between the statistic and the population parameter. If there is some observed difference, than it is merely due to fluctuations in sampling from the same population. The null hypothesis is denoted by $H_0$. A hypothesis that contradicts the null hypothesis is known as alternative hypothesis and is donated by $H_1$.

The two hypothesis are such that if $H_0$ is true, $H_1$ is false and vice versa. Thus, to test whether the population mean $\mu = \mu_0$ where $\mu_0$ is a definite value, we have to note the following:

(a)     Null hypothesis $H_0 : \mu = \mu_0$

(b)     Alternative hypothesis maybe $H_1 = \mu \neq \mu_0$  $H_1 : \mu > \mu_0$  or  $H_1 : \mu < \mu_0$

The alternative hypothesis:

$H_1 = \mu \neq \mu_0$   implying that $\mu > \mu_0$  and  $\mu < \mu_0$ is called a two - tailed alternative.

The hypothesis $H_1 : \mu > \mu_0$   is called the right - tailed alternative and the hypothesis $H_1 : \mu < \mu_0$ is called the left - tailed alternative

While testing the above hypothesis we may come across two types of errors: Type I and Type II errors

1.      H0 is true and if it is rejected ,it is Type I error.

2.      H0 is false and if it is accepted, it is Type II error.

## Critical region

The sampling distribution of mean x of a sample of size n drawn from a normal population with mean m and standard deviation $\sigma$ is a normal distribution with mean m and standard deviation $\dfrac{\sigma}{\sqrt{n}}$. Therefore if we write then $Z = \dfrac{X-\mu}{\sigma}$ then Z is a standard normal variable with mean 0 and S.D equal to 1. If this statistic Z lies between -1.96 and + 1.96 then we have 95 % confidence that the hypothesis is true, i.e. P(-1.96$\leq$ Z$\leq$1.96)=0.95, we note the following: if / z / > 1.96 , then the hypothesis is rejected at 5 % level of significance. The value of z inside the range -1.96 to 1.96 is known as region of acceptance of the hypothesis. The values -1.96 and 1.96 are known as critical values at 5 % level of significance

The above explanation gives rise to the following two sided test decision.

## Standard Error(SE)

SE is used as an instrument in all the hypothesis or tests of significance. It is useful in finding the limits known as confidence limits within which concerned parameters are supposed and expected to lie. Testing of hypothesis mean may relate to the following categories:

a)      Sampling of variables with respect to large samples where the sample size n $\geq$ 30.

b)      Sampling of attributes

c)      Sampling of variables with respect to small samples where the sample size n < 30.

When a sample is drawn from an infinite population without replacement, then the formula for the SE of the sample mean is $\dfrac{\sigma}{\sqrt{n}}$ .

But for a finite population of size N from where a sample of size n is drawn without replacement the formula for the SE is $\dfrac{\sigma}{\sqrt{n}}\sqrt{\dfrac{N-n}{N-1}}$ .

This is because a correction factor $\sqrt{\dfrac{N-n}{N-1}}$ is used as the value of the sampling fraction becomes greater than 0.05 (population size N being finite)

Standard error( large sample test)

While testing the significance of statistics such as mean, median, SD etc. in case of large samples, standard error is used. The following are the formulae for calculating SE relating to the sampling of variables (large samples) and also for the sampling of attributes (proportions)

With reference to infinite population relating to variables, the following aspects should be noted.

(i)     The SE of the sample mean($\bar{x}$) is $\dfrac{\sigma}{\sqrt{n}}$ where $\sigma$ is the SD of the population and n is the sample size

(ii)    the SE of sample standard deviation (s) is $\sqrt{\dfrac{\sigma^2}{2n}}$ .

(iii)   The SE of the difference of the mean $\bar{x}_1$ and $\bar{x}_2$ of two samples of size $n_1$ and $n_2$ respectively drawn from the population having standard deviation $\sigma_1$ and $\sigma_2$ respectively is $\sqrt{\dfrac{\sigma_1^2}{n_1}+\dfrac{\sigma_2^2}{n_2}}$

(iv)    For calculating the SE to test the significance of the difference between $\sigma_1$ and $\sigma_2$ of two samples of size $n_1$ and $n_2$  the formula is $\sqrt{\dfrac{\sigma_1^2}{2n_1}+\dfrac{\sigma_2^2}{2n_2}}$ .

(v)     Note for finite population, the SE of sample mean is $\dfrac{\sigma}{\sqrt{n}}\sqrt{\dfrac{N-n}{N-1}}$ .

With respect to sampling of attributes, the following details should be noted.

(i)     The SE of sample proportion p is $\sqrt{\dfrac{PQ}{N}}$ where P is the population proportion and Q is 1-p and n is the sample size

(ii)    SE of the sample proportion P, in the case of finite population of size N is $\sqrt{\dfrac{PQ}{N}}\sqrt{\dfrac{N-n}{N-1}}$

(iii)   The SE for testing the significance of the difference between two proportions $P_1$ and $P_2$ of two random samples of size $n_1$ and $n_2$ drawn from two populations with proportions P1 and P2 is $\sqrt{pq}\left[\dfrac{n_1+n_2}{n_1 n_2}\right]$ where $p = \left[\dfrac{n1\,p1 + n2\,p2}{n1\,n2}\right]$ and q = 1-p

For finding the interval in which a population parameter such as a mean, we find confidence limits with a certain degree of probability and confidence. Hence SE is used to determine these two confidence limits within which the parameter is expected to lie. While calculating the confidence interval and confidence limits, the basis is the central limit theorem pertaining to the sampling distribution. This theorem states that if x̄ is the mean of a random sample of size n drawn from a population having a mean μ and S.D σ, then the sampling distribution of sample mean is approximately a normal distribution with mean m and S.D. equal to SE of x , provided the sample size n is sufficiently large (where n ≥ 30)

Further, the variate Z = $\dfrac{\bar{x} - ?}{\frac{\sigma}{\sqrt{n}}}$ has a standard normal distribution with a mean equal to 0 and S.D. equal to 1.

The confidence interval defined by two confidence limits is expressed in terms of a specified confidence or probability ratio such as 95%, 95. 45%, 99% and 99.73% for estimating the true value of the population parameter.

The confidence limits for population means μ can be stated as under:

(a)     95 % confidence limits are x̄ ± 1.96 (SE)

(b)     99 % confidence limits are x̄ ± 2.58 (SE)

(c)     95.45 % confidence limits are x̄ ± 2 (SE)

(d)     99.73 % confidence limits are $\bar{x} \pm 3$ (SE)

Similarly, the confidence limits for population proportion P can be stated as:

(a)     95 % confidence limits are p $\pm$ 1.96 (SE)

(b)     99 % confidence limits are p $\pm$ 2.58 (SE)

(c)     95.45 % confidence limits are p $\pm$ 2 (SE)

(d)     99.73 confidence limits are p $\pm$ 3 (SE)

## Right tailed test and Left tailed test

(a)     For R.T.T.

   $H0 : \mu = \mu_0$

   $H1 : \mu > \mu_0$

   Critical region is the shaded area K = 0.05, at 5% level

(b)     For L.T.T.

   $H0 : \mu = \mu_0$

   $H1 : \mu > \mu_0$

   Critical region is the shaded region where K = 0.05, at 5% level

**Table showing the level of significance of critical values**

| Level of significance | Two = tailed | R.T.T. | L.T.T. |
|---|---|---|---|
| 1% | $|Zk| = 2.58$ | Zk= 2.33 | Zk= 2.33 |
| 5% | $|Zk| = 1.96$ | Zk= 1.645 | Zk= 1.645 |
| 10% | $|Zk| = 1.645$ | Zk= 1.28 | Zk= 1.28 |

## Problem 1:

A population consists of 5 members 2, 3, 6, 8, 11. Find all possible distinct samples of size two that can be drawn from this population. Varify that the population mean is equal to the mean of the sampling distribution.

Solution: Here $\mu = \dfrac{2 + 3 + 6 + 8 + 11}{5} = 6$

The number of samples of size 2 = 5C2 = 10

These samples are (2,3), (2,6), (2,8), (2,11), (3,6), (3,8), (3,11), (6,8), (6,11), (8,11)

Their respective means are

2.5, 4.5, 6.5, 4.5, 5.5, 7, 7, 8.5, 9.5

Mean of this sampling distribution is

$$= \frac{(2.5)+4+5+(6.5)+(4.5)+(5.5)+7+7+(8.5)+(9 5)}{10}$$

$$= \frac{60}{10}$$

$$= 6$$

This is the same as the population mean $\mu$. Hence it is verified

## Problem 2:

Given that n = 64, $\bar{x}$ = 32, population S.D. $\sigma$ = 3, test the hypothesis $\mu$ = 33

Solution:

Here, $Z = \frac{|\bar{x}-\mu|}{SE}$, where

$H_0$ $\mu$= 33, $H_1$ : $\mu \neq 33$ (two = tailed test)

$$SE = \frac{\sigma}{\sqrt{n}} = \frac{3}{8}, \quad Z = \frac{/32-33/}{SE} = \frac{8}{3} = 2.67 > 1.96$$

Therefore, we reject the hypothesis. The population mean cannot be accepted as 33.

## Problem 3:

A group of 50 students from a large class was selected at random. The average age was found to be 21.5 years with a S.D. of 4. Test the hypothesis that the population mean can be taken as 22 years.

Solution: $Z = \dfrac{|21.5-22.0|}{SE}$

Where, $SE = \dfrac{\sigma}{\sqrt{n}} = \dfrac{4}{\sqrt{50}} = \dfrac{4}{7.07} = 0.566$

$Z = \dfrac{|\,|\,21.5-22.0| = 0.88}{0.566} < 1.96\,|$

The difference is not significant at the 5% level. Hence, accept the hypothesis. The average age of all students in the large class can be taken as 22 years.

## Problem 4:

A sample of size 121 has been drawn from a large population. If the mean of the sample is 28, test whether the sample belongs to a normal population whose mean is 30 and variance 16.

Solution:

$H_0 : \mu = 30$

$H_1 : \mu \neq 30$ (two = tailed test)

$SE = \dfrac{\sigma}{\sqrt{n}} = \dfrac{4}{11}$

$Z = \dfrac{|\,|\bar{x} - \square|}{SE} = \dfrac{|\,|28-30|}{4/11} = \dfrac{|\,2 \times 11}{4} = 5.25 > 1.96$, difference is significant

We reject the null hypothesis at 5% level of significance.

## Problem 5:

A manufacturer ordered ball bearings of diameter 10mm. A random sample of 100 bearings were taken from the shipment. It was found that the mean diameter was 10.02 mm with a S.D. of 0.28mm. Test the significance at 5% level.

Solution:

$SE = \dfrac{\sigma}{\sqrt{n}} = \dfrac{0.28}{\sqrt{100}} = 0.028$

$H_0: \mu = 10$

$H_1: \mu \neq 10$

$$Z = \frac{||\bar{x} - \mu|}{SE} = \frac{||10.02 - 10.0|}{0.028} = 0.71 < 1.96$$

The difference is not significant at 5% level. We accept the hypothesis. Therefore, the shipment can be accepted.

## Problem 6:

A particular make of electric bulb has a mean life of 1400 hours with a S.D. of 64 hours. A random sample of 100 bulbs when tested showed a mean life of 1250 hours. Explain the quality of the bulb at 5 % level of significance.

**Solution:**

$H_0: \mu = 1400$

$H_1 : \mu \neq 1400$ (Supposing the quality has deteriorated)

Here it is a one = tailed test

$$SE = \frac{\sigma}{\sqrt{n}} = \frac{64}{\sqrt{100}} = 6.4$$

$$Z = \frac{|1250 - 1400|}{SE} = 23.4375 > 1.96 \text{ at the 5\% level.}$$

We reject the hypothesis. Therefore, the quality of the bulb has deteriorated.

## Problem 7:

From a large consignment of mangoes, 400 were selected, of which 40 were found to be spoilt. Estimate the percentage of spoiled mangoes in the consignment and find the limits within which the percentage lies.

Solution:

Regarding the proportion of success we have.

$$SE = \sqrt{\frac{PQ}{N}}$$

Here $P = \frac{40}{400} = 0.1$, therefore $q = 0.9$

$$SE = \sqrt{\frac{0.1 \times 0.9}{400}} = \sqrt{\frac{0.09}{400}} = 0.015$$

Therefore, the limits for finding the percentage of spoiled mangoes are:

[p+3(SE)] x 100 and [p-3(SE)] x 100

i.e. [0.1+3(0.015)] x 100 and [0.1-3(0.015)]x100

i.e. ( 0.145)x100 and (0.055)x100

i.e. 14.5% and 5.5%

## Problem 8:

Out of 1,000 males selected at random, 600 are found to be smokers in city X and out of 900 males selected at random from city Y, 450 are smokers. Is there a significant difference between cities X and Y as far as Male Smokers are concerned?

Solution:

Here,

$P_1 = \dfrac{600}{1000} = 0.6$, $n_1 = 100$

$P_2 = \dfrac{450}{900} = 0.5$, $n_2 = 900$

$P = \dfrac{n_1 P_1 + n_2 P_2}{n_1 + n_2} = \dfrac{1000\,(0.6) + 900\,(0.5)}{1000 + 900} = 0.55$, $q = 0.45$

$= \dfrac{600 + 450}{1900} = \dfrac{1050}{1900} = \dfrac{21}{38}$

$q = 1 - p = 1 - \dfrac{21}{38} = \dfrac{17}{38}$

$SE = \sqrt{pq\left(\dfrac{1}{n_1} + \dfrac{1}{n_2}\right)} = \sqrt{\dfrac{21}{38} \times \dfrac{17}{38}\left(\dfrac{1}{1000} + \dfrac{1}{900}\right)} = 0.023$

$\therefore \dfrac{difference}{SE} = \dfrac{P_1 - P_2}{SE} = \dfrac{0.6 - 0.5}{0.023} = 4.3478 = 4.35 > 1.96$

∵The difference is significant at 5% level of significance.

Hence, there is a significant difference in the smoking habits of males in cities X and Y.

## Problem 9:

At a certain competitive examination, 640 male students and 560 female students appeared. The mean and standard deviation in the marks secured by male students were 56.4 and 18.2 respectively, whereas those of female students were 60.2 and 18.8 respectively. Test the significance of the difference in performance.

## Solution:

Here $n_1 = 640$      $n_2 = 560$

     $\sigma_1 = 18.2$      $\sigma_2 = 18.8$

     $\bar{x}_1 = 56.4$      $\bar{x}_2 = 60$

$$SE = \sqrt{\frac{\sigma_1^2}{n_1} + \frac{\sigma_2^2}{n_2}} = \sqrt{\frac{(18.2)^2}{640} + \frac{(18.8)^2}{560}}$$

$$= \sqrt{\frac{331.25}{640} + \frac{353.44}{560}} = \sqrt{0.518 + 0.631}$$

$$= \sqrt{1.149} = 1.072$$

Now, $\dfrac{Difference}{SE} = \dfrac{|56.4 - 60.2|}{1.072} = \dfrac{|56.4 - 60.2|}{1.072} = 3.8$

$= 3.54 > 2.58$

Therefore, the difference is significant at the 1% level of significance. Hence there is a difference between the performance of male students and that of female students.

## Parametric tests

Parameters of a population such as mean, standard deviation, variance etc play a significant role for the purpose of estimating the same on the basis of samples drawn at random. Therefore parametric tests of hypothesis dealing with large and as well as small samples are of much relevance in research.

These tests comprise of Z test based on normal probability distribution, f- test, $X^2$ test and f- test. $X^2$ test is also known as a test of goodness of fit. When $X^2$ test is used as a test of independence it becomes a non- parametric test. Examples, in this connection have been explained under nonparametric tests.

Z test is used for the purpose of testing the significance of measures such as mean, standard deviation, variance. In the case of large samples, we can compare the mean $\bar{x}$ of a sample drawn from a population with the hypothesised (assumed) mean ($\mu$) of the population

## t- test

In the case of small samples, where the sample size is less than 30 members, appropriate parametric test is the t-test which is based on t distribution. This test can be used for testing the significance of a sample mean or for testing the difference between the means of two small samples on the basis of sample variance in the absence of information about the population variance. Further, given two related samples, we use the difference test which is known as the paired t- test, for testing the significance of the difference between the means of the two related samples. This test is also used for testing the significance of simple or partial correlation coefficient. The procedure for testing consists in calculating the value of t on the basis of a given sample data and then comparing the calculated value of t with specific value of t, given in the table with reference to the level of significance and the pertaining degrees of freedom.

## Problem 10:

The following data pertains to the heights in cms of 10 persons selected at random from a village. Find out whether it would be reasonable to suppose the mean height of that village population as 182 cms. (Given $t_{0.05}$=2.26 for 9 d-f) 185, 181, 173, 177, 176, 174, 189, 185, 183, 177.

**Solution:**

| Height (X) | X - $\bar{x}$ | $(X - \bar{x})^2$ |
|:----------:|:-------------:|:------------------:|
| 185 | 5 | 25 |
| 181 | 1 | 1 |
| 173 | -7 | 49 |
| 177 | -3 | 9 |

| 176 | -4 | 16 |
| 174 | -6 | 36 |
| 189 | 9 | 81 |
| 185 | 5 | 25 |
| 183 | 3 | 9 |
| 177 | -3 | 9 |
| 1800 | 0 | 260 |

$$\bar{x} = \frac{1800}{10} = 180, \ n = 10, \ \mu = 182$$

$$s = \sqrt{\frac{\Sigma(X-\bar{x})^2}{n-1}} = \sqrt{\frac{260}{9}} = \sqrt{28.89} = 5.37$$

$$t = \frac{|\bar{X} - \mu|}{s}\sqrt{n} = \frac{/180-182/}{5.37}\sqrt{10}$$

$$= (0.372)(3.16) = 1.177$$

Comparing the calculated value of t with the table value, we find $1.177 < 2.26$.

Therefore, the difference is not significant.

Therefore, it would be reasonable to suppose the population mean as 182cms.

## Problem 11:

The following data relates to 2 samples drawn from two different normal populations. Test whether both the samples can be considered as belonging to the same population.

Application of t test for testing the significance of the difference between 2 sample means.

| Sample I | $X_1$ | 11 | 15 | 18 | 11 | 15 | 13 | 19 | 12 | 10 | 16 | | |
| Sample II | $X_2$ | 13 | 18 | 14 | 12 | 15 | 11 | 13 | 18 | 17 | 19 | 13 | 17 |

**Solution:**

Here, $n_1 = 10$, $n_2 = 12$

$$\therefore t = \frac{|\bar{x}_1 - \bar{x}_2|}{s} \sqrt{\frac{n_1 n_2}{n_1 + n_2}}$$

$$= \frac{|14 - 15|}{2.88} \sqrt{\frac{120}{22}}$$

$$= 0.8106$$

$$S = \sqrt{\frac{(x_1 - x_1)^2 + (x_2 - x_2)^2}{n_1 + n_2 - 2}}$$

$$= \sqrt{\frac{86 + 80}{20}}$$

$$= \sqrt{8.3}$$

$$= 2.881$$

Table value

$T_{0.05} = 2.086$

For 20d.f

Comparing, $0.8106 < 2.086$

The difference between the sample means is not significant.

---

## Problem 12:

---

The following data shows the performance of 11 students in economics in 2 different tests conducted before providing them with coaching and after 10 weeks coaching. Find out whether the coaching has benefitted the students or not.

| Marks before coaching | 47 | 53 | 64 | 73 | 58 | 22 | 40 | 45 | 64 | 71 | 44 |
|---|---|---|---|---|---|---|---|---|---|---|---|
| Marks after coaching | 53 | 51 | 62 | 78 | 85 | 77 | 33 | 49 | 61 | 85 | 57 |

**Solution:**

(Given $t_{0.05}$=2.23 for 10 d-f)

| Before coaching | After coaching | d | $(d - \bar{d})^2$ |
|---|---|---|---|
| 47 | 53 | 6 | 16 |
| 53 | 51 | -2 | 144 |
| 64 | 62 | -2 | 144 |
| 73 | 78 | 5 | 25 |
| 58 | 85 | 27 | 289 |
| 22 | 77 | 55 | 2025 |
| 40 | 33 | -7 | 289 |
| 45 | 49 | 4 | 36 |
| 64 | 61 | -3 | 169 |
| 71 | 85 | 14 | 16 |
| 44 | 57 | 13 | 9 |
| | | 110 | 3162 |

$$\bar{d} = \frac{\Sigma d}{n} = \frac{110}{11} = 10$$

$$t = \frac{\bar{d}}{s}\sqrt{n} = 1.865 \quad \text{i.e. } t = \frac{10}{17.78}\sqrt{11} = 1.865$$

$$s = \sqrt{\frac{(d-\bar{d})^2}{n-1}} = \sqrt{\frac{3162}{11-1}}$$

$$= 17.78$$

Comparing the calculated value of t with the table value, at 5% level of significance, we find 1.865 < 2.23.

Therefore, the difference is not significant.

Therefore, coaching has not been effective.

Chi-square test(x2 test)

X2 test is a parametric test

X2 test for testing the significance of population variance (test of homogenecity)

To test whether a random sample has been drawn from a normal population, with the respective parameters mean m and variance $\sigma 2$ we calculate X2 using the formula

$X2 = \frac{\sigma_s{}^2}{\sigma^2} (n-1)$

Where   $\sigma^2$= variance of the population

$\sigma_s{}^2$=variance of the sample

n – 1=Sample size(n) minus one

---

## Problem13:

---

The following data shows the marks obtained by a random sample of 10 students (selected from a normal population) in mathematics at the B.Sc examination. Find out whether the variance in the marks of the concerned population is 80

| Roll No. | Marks (X) |
|----------|-----------|
| 1 | 55 |
| 2 | 59 |
| 3 | 63 |
| 4 | 68 |
| 5 | 56 |
| 6 | 73 |
| 7 | 82 |
| 8 | 76 |
| 9 | 64 |
| 10 | 74 |
|  | 670 |

## Working

| Marks X | 55 | 59 | 63 | 65 | 56 | 73 | 82 | 76 | 64 | 74 |
|---------|-----|-----|-----|-----|-----|-----|-----|-----|-----|-----|
| $(X - \bar{x})^2$ | 144 | 64 | 16 | 1 | 121 | 36 | 225 | 81 | 9 | 49 |

$\bar{x} = \dfrac{670}{10} = 67$

$\Sigma(X - \bar{x})^2 = 746$

$\text{Variance} = \dfrac{\Sigma(X - \bar{x})^2}{n-1} = \dfrac{746}{9} = 82.89 = \sigma_s^2$

$X^2 = \dfrac{\sigma_s^2}{\sigma^2}(n-1)$

$\quad = \dfrac{82.89}{80}(10-1)$

$\quad = 9.325$

The table value at $X^2$ at 5% level of significance for 9 degrees of freedom is 16.92. Now the calculated value 9.325 is less than 16.92

Therefore, the null hypothesis is accepted .This implies that the statement that the sample could have been selected from the population whose variance is 80, is correct.

## Exercise VII

Questions:

1. Explain the following (a) Null hypothesis (b) alternative hypothesis (c) level of significance, two tailed test.

2. Write an explanatory note on the limitations of tests of significance with reference to large samples.

3. Discuss the basic principles of large samples with special reference to sampling for attributes

4. Random sample of 400 items has a mean of 7.2. Can this sample be regarded as belonging to a large population having a mean of 7.5 and SD of 1.5 2.

5. The percentage of males in a random sample of 500 persons from a large town is 62 %. Test whether the statement that the ratio of males to the population of that town is 2:3 is statistically justified.

6. In 324 throws of a six faced die, odd points appeared 181 times. Would you say that the die is fair? State carefully the property on which you base your conclusion.

7. A 1000 mangoes are taken from a large consignment, of which 100 are found to be bad. Estimate the percentage of bad mangoes in the consignment and assign the limits within which the percentage lies.

8. Random sample of 500 pineapples was taken from a large consignment and 65 were found to be bad. Show that the SE of the proportion of bad ones in a sample of this size is 0.015 and deduce that the percentage of bad pineapples in the consignment almost certainly lies between 8.5 and 1.75.

9. The mean of simple samples of sizes 1000 and 2000 are 67.5 and 68.0 inches respectively. Can the samples be regarded as drawn from the same population of standard deviation of 2.5 inches.

10.    The mean of a random sample of 100 individuals from a population is 64.3. The standard deviation of the sample is 2.7. Would it be unreasonable to suppose that the mean of the population is 60.

11.    In a large city, 800 out of a random sample of 1000 men were found to be smokers. After a big increase in the tax on tobacco, another random sample of 1200 men in the same city included 800 smokers. Test the significance.

12.    Random sample of thousand farms in a certain your give an average yield of 2000 lb with a standard deviation of 192 lb. Random sample of 1000 farms in the following year give a anaverage yield of 2100 lb per acre with a standard deviation of 202 lb. Are these data consistent with hypothesis that average yields in the country were the same in these two years?

13.    A random sample of 200 villages was taken from Kanpur district and the average population per village was found to be 420 with a SD of 50. Another random sample of 200 villages from the same district gave an average population of 484 village with a SD of 60. Is the difference between the averages of the two samples statistically significant?

14.    Here are the results of intelligence test on two groups of boys and girls. Examine whether the difference is significant

| Girls | Mean 84 | S.D =10 | N=121 |
| Boys | Mean 81 | S.D =12 | N=81 |

15.    500 articles were selected at random from a batch containing 10000 articles and 34 were found to be defective. How many defective articles would you reasonably expect to find in the whole batch?

16.    Random sample of size 32 was drawn from a normal population and sample standard deviation was found to be 1.38. Using 1 % level of significance decide if it would be reasonable to adopt the value unity for the population standard deviation.

17.    Two samples were drawn from a recent survey each containing 500 hamlets. In the first sample the mean population per hamlet was found to be 100 with a SD of 20, while in the second sample the mean population

was 120 with a SD of 15. Do you find the averages of the samples to be statistically significant?

18.   Random sample of size 100 has a mean of 15, the population variance being 25. Find an interval estimate of the population means with a confidence level of i) 99% and ii)95%.

19.   A population consists of 5 numbers 2,3,6,8,11. Consider all possible samples of size two which can be drawn with replacement from this population. Calculate the SE of sample means.

20.    The values of a characteristic x of a population containing six units are given by 2,3,6,1,7,3. Take all possible samples of size two and verify that the mean of the population is exactly equal to the mean of the sample means.

21.   A simple random sample of size 5 is drawn without replacement from a finite population consisting of 41 units. If the population SD is 6.25, find the standard error of sample mean.

22.   Random sample of size 10 from a normal population gives the value 64, 72, 65, 70, 68, 71, 65, 62, 66, 76. If the standard error of the sample mean is, $\sqrt{0.7}$ find 95 % confidence interval for the population mean. Also find the population variance.

23.   Random sample of 100 articles is taken from a large batch of articles containing 5 defective articles. Set up 96% confidence limits for the proportion of defective articles in the batch. If the batch contains 2696 articles, set up 95% confidence interval for the proportion of defective articles.

24.   10 life insurance policies in a sample of 200 taken out of 50,000 were found to be insured for less than Rs5000. How many policies can be reasonably expected to be insured for less than 5000 in the whole lot at a 95 % confidence level?

25.   Explain the following

Hypothesis: null hypothesis and alternat hypothesis

Standard error

Large sample test

Level of significance and critical region

Right tailed and left tailed test

Type 1 and type 2 errors

Small sample test

Parametric test

26 The following data shows the distribution of wages amongst 100 workers. Find the arithmetic mean and test whether it is significantly differs from 50(use large sample test)

| Wages (in Rs) | 10-25 | 23-40 | 40-55 | 55-70 | 70-85 | 85-100 |
|---|---|---|---|---|---|---|
| No.of workers | 6 | 20 | 44 | 26 | 3 | 1 |

27. In a certain sample of 400 items the mean is 18.2 and SD is 2.4. Is the mean significantly different from 17?

28. In a large city, 500 men out of 1200 men were found to be smokers. Does this information imply that the majority of men in the city are smokers?

29. A sample of 1000 persons selected from a large city show the percentage of males as 52 %. Is there sufficient evidence to conclude that males and females are equal in number?

30. Random sample of 400 pineapples from a large consignment showed 55 rotten pineapples. Estimate the percentage of rotten pineapple in the entire consignment. Find 95 % confidence limits for the percentage of rotten pineapples in the consignment.

31. With reference to the following data find out whether the two arithmetic means of the samples significantly differ.

I: mean=12.45 S.D=2.38 n=500 sample

II: mean=14.18 S.D=3.12 n=600 sample

32. Consumer survey carried out in two cities A and B in regard to the consumer preferences for a particular brand of tea, indicated 64 % and 67 %. If the random sample of consumers in A and B was 400 and 500 respectively examine the significance of the difference in preferences in the two cities at 5 % level.

33. A random sample of 100 villages from a certain district showed the average population as 315 per village with SD of 25. Another random sample of 80 villages from the same district show the average population as 240 per village with SD of 18. Is the difference between the two average populations significant at 1 % level of significance?

34. Two samples drawn from a population with SD as 4, provided the following results: sample 1: mean= 75, sample size= 20. Sample 2: mean= 55, sample size = 180. Examine whether the mean of the first sample significantly differs from the combined mean of both the samples at 1 % level.

35. Random sample of 11 students from a population indicated the sample mean as 56. If the estimate of the population SD is 3.4 are we justified in supposing the population mean marks as 55?( use t test to examine at 5 % level of significance)

36. A sample of size 15 has arithmetic mean 62 and SD as 5.4. Does this sample belong to a population where arithmetic mean is 60?

37. A certain stimulus administered to each of 15 patients indicated the following changes in the blood pressure

4, 1, 7,-2 ,4 ,1 ,3 ,4 ,2 ,3 ,-2 ,5 ,8 ,-4 , 2

Does the stimulus bring about an increase in blood pressure? Examine at 5 % level of significance.

38. Five persons complete a piece of work in 54, 68, 72, 46, 50 seconds respectively by using method A and another group of 4 persons complete the same piece of work in 66, 76, 70, 75 by using method B. Is method B preferable to method A? (use f test to verify whether the variance in terms of time is the same in the two groups of persons)

# Testing of hypothesis (II)

## Chi-square test

**X² - test as a non parametric or distribution free test**: when there does not arise the necessity of specific assumption about the type of population, then X² test can be used as (i) a test of goodness of fit. (ii) as a test of independence. The degree of freedom for finding the table value is sample: size n minus 1 = (n - 1)

**X² test as a test of goodness of fit**: when a given data is classified on the basis of a single attribute then the X2 Test becomes a test of goodness of fit. In research problems in the area of marketing research and psychology, the usual assumptions applicable in the case of parametric tests, are not valid. Hence such problems are dealt with as non-parametric.

**Problem 1**: A manufacturer of bicycles introduces three different types A, B, C and as per the demand pattern sells usually 80, 70 and 60 per week. To improve the sales it has introduced certain modifications in these three types of bicycles and the demand changes to 95, 75, 64.

The company wants to know whether the demand pattern shows significant change.

| Type | Expected sales | Observed sales |
|------|---------------|----------------|
| A | 80 | 95 |
| B | 70 | 75 |
| C | 60 | 64 |

**Solutions:**

Null hypothesis: there is no significant difference in sales.

**Calculations:**

| 0 | E | $(0 - E)^2/E$ |
|---|---|---------------|
| 95 | 80 | 2.8125 |
| 75 | 70 | 0.3571 |
| 64 | 60 | 0.2667 |
| | | 3.4365 |

The table value of $X^2$ at 5% level of significance for 2 degrees of freedom (3 - 1) is 5.991.

Here, $X2 = \Sigma \left[ \frac{(0-E)^2}{E} \right] = 3.4365$

On comparing the calculated value of X2 with the table value we find that 3.4365 < 5.991.

The null hypothesis is accepted. Hence there is no significant difference in the demand pattern.

Problems of $X^2$ test: as a test of independence.

**Problem 8**: A random sample of 1,280 persons from a small town provided the following information

| Effects of cholera | Inoculated | Non inoculated |
|--------------------|-----------|----------------|
| Attacked | 200 | 120 |
| Not Attacked | 400 | 560 |

Find out whether inoculaticn is effective in controlling the disease.

**Solution:**

| | Inoculated A | Not inoculated a | Total |
|---|---|---|---|
| Attacked B | 0.200 = (AB) E : 150 | 0.120 (aB) E : 170 | 230 = (B) |
| Not attacked b | 0.400 = (Ab) E : 450 | 0.560 = (ab) E : 510 | 960 = (b) |
| Total | 600 = (A) | 680 = (a) | 1280 = N |

Hypothesis: A and B are independent

We had expected $(AB) = \frac{(A) \ (B)}{N}$

$$= \frac{(600) \ (320)}{1280} = 150$$

| 0 | E | $\frac{(0 - E)^2}{E}$ |
|---|---|---|
| 200 | 150 | $\frac{50^2}{150} = \frac{2500}{150} = 16.67$ |
| 400 | 450 | $\frac{2500}{450} = 5.56$ |
| 120 | 170 | $\frac{2500}{170} = 14.71$ |
| 560 | 510 | $\frac{2500}{510} = 4.90$ $X^2 = 41.84$(Calculated value) |

Table value: $X^2{}_{0.5} = 3.84$

$X^2 = \Sigma \left[ \frac{(0-E)^2}{E} \right] = 41.84$

Now 41.84 > 3.84

**Remark:**

On comparing the calculated value with the table value, we find that the difference between 0 and E is significant.

Therefore, the hypothesis is rejected, therefore, A and B are dependent.

Therefore, inoculation is effective in preventing the attack of cholera.

**Problem 3**: A new type of cough syrup was claimed to be effective in controlling cough instantly. In an experiment on 100 persons having severe cough, 50 persons were given the new cough syrup and the other 50 were given sugar syrup. It was observed that the 100 persons showed reactions as under:

|  | Provided relief | Adverse reaction | Not effective | Total |
|---|---|---|---|---|
| Cough syrup | 28 | 9 | 13 | 50 |
| Sugar syrup | 23 | 3 | 24 | 50 |
| Total | 51 | 12 | 37 | 100 |

Test the hypothesis that the new type of cough syrup is no better than sugar syrup

( Given $X^2_{0.5}$ = 5.491 for d.f. = 2 )

**Solution:**

The following are the calculations

## Cough syrup

| Observed value | Expected value | (0-E)2 | (0-E)2/E |
|---|---|---|---|
| 28 | 51 x 52/100=25.5 | (2.5)2 | 0.245 |
| 9 | 12 x 50/100=6.0 | (3)2 | 1.500 |
| 13 | 37 x 50/100=18.5 | (-5.5)2 | 1.635 |

## Sugar syrup

| | | | |
|---|---|---|---|
| 23 | 51 x 50/100 =25.5 | $(-2.5)^2$ | 0.245 |
| 3 | 12 x 50/100=6.0 | $(-3)^2$ | 1.095 |
| 24 | 37 x 50/100=18.5 | $(5.5)^2$ | 1.635 |

$X^2 = \Sigma[(0 - E)2 / E] = 6.36$

Degrees of freedom = (No. of rows - 1) (No. of cols. - 1) = (2 - 1) (3 - 1) = 2

The table value of chi-square for two degrees of freedom at 5% level of significance is 5.991, i.e. X2 0.05 = 5.991, df = 2. On comparing the calculated value with the table value we find that

6.36 > 5.991

Hence, the difference is significant.

This implies that the new cough syrup is better than the sugar syrup.

## F-test (Variance – Ratio test)

If $S_1^2$ and $S_2^2$ are the respective variances of two independent samples of sizes $n_1$ and $n_2$ then the variance - ratio denoted by F is

$F = S_1^2$ where $S_1^2$ is a higher variance

$\overline{\phantom{S}}$

$S_2^2$

Here $S_1^2 = \dfrac{\Sigma (X_1 - \bar{x})^2}{n_1 - 1}$ and $S_2^2 = \dfrac{\Sigma (X_2 - \bar{x})^2}{n_2 - 1}$

and where $X_1$ and $X_2$ are the variables corresponding to the samples and $X_1$ and $X_2$ are the Arithmetic means of $X_1$ and $X_2$ respectively.

The testing procedure consists in comparing the calculated value of F with the table value of F , at 5% level of significance for $n_1 - 1$ and $n_2 - 1$ degrees of freedom.

Interpretation:

If $F_{cal} > F_{0.05}$ the variance ratio is significant and $H_0$ is rejected.

If $F_{cal} < F_{0.05}$ the variance ratio is not significant and $H_0$ is accepted.

Where $H_0$ represents the null hypothesis.

F – test

Problem 4: The following are two samples:

| Sample I | 11 | 15 | 18 | 11 | 15 | 13 | 19 | 12 | 10 | 16 | | |
| --- | --- | --- | --- | --- | --- | --- | --- | --- | --- | --- | --- | --- |
| Sample II | 13 | 18 | 14 | 12 | 15 | 11 | 13 | 18 | 17 | 19 | 13 | 17 |

Test whether they belong to the same population.

Solution:

$\bar{X}_1 = 14$, $\bar{X}_2 = 15$

$S^2_1 = \dfrac{86}{9} = 9.556$

$S^2_2 = \dfrac{80}{11} = 7.273$

Therefore, $F = \dfrac{S^2_1}{S^2_2} = \dfrac{9.556}{7.273} = 1.314$

Table value $F_{0.05} = 2.91$

for d.f. (9, 11)

Comparing, $1.314 < 2.91$

Therefore, not significant, both the samples can be said to belong to the same population.

## Exercise VIII

### Questions :

1.  The following table shows price increase and decrease in markets where credit squeeze is in operation and where it is not in operation.

| Credit squeeze | Price decrease | Price increase | Total |
|---|---|---|---|
| In operation | 862 | 10 | 872 |
| Not in operation | 582 | 18 | 600 |
| Total | 1444 | 28 | 1472 |

Find whether the credit squeeze has been effective in checking price increase [$X^2 = 6.6$ ; $x^2_{0.05}$ for $v = 1 = 3.841$ credit squeeze is effective in checking price increase]

2.  The following table shows the results of inoculation against cholera in a certain tea estate.

| | Not Attacked | Attacked | Total |
|---|---|---|---|
| Inoculated | 267 | 37 | 394 |
| Not Inoculated | 757 | 155 | 912 |
| | 1024 | 192 | 1216 |

Find out whether there is any significant association between inoculation and attack, given the following value of $X^2$ at 5% level.

| Degrees of freedom | 1 | 2 | 3 | 4 |
|---|---|---|---|---|
| Value of $x^2$ | 3.841 | 5.991 | 7.815 | 9.488 |

[$X^2 = 3.99$ ; $x^2_{0.5}$ for $v = 1$ < 3.841 Inoculation and attack are associated]

3. The following data relates to the sales in a time of trade depression, of a certain proprietary article in wide demand. Do the data suggest that the sales are significantly affected bt the depression?

| District where sales are | Districts not hit by depression | Districts hit by depression | Total |
|---|---|---|---|
| Satisfactory | 250 | 80 | 330 |
| Not satisfactory | 140 | 30 | 170 |
| Totals | 390 | 110 | 500 |

$[X^2 = 2.53 ; x^2_{0.05} = 3.84$ Hypothesis holds good]

4. Two sample polls of votes for two candidates A and B for a public office are taken one from among residents of urban area and the other one from residents of rural area. The results are given below. Examine whether the nature of the area is related to voting preference in the election.

| Votes for area | A | B | Total |
|---|---|---|---|
| Rural | 620 | 380 | 1000 |
| Urban | 550 | 450 | 1000 |
| Total | 1170 | 830 | 2000 |

$[X^2 = 10.6 ;$ Table value of $x^2$ at 5% level for v = 1 k 3.84 Hypothesis does not hold good ]

5. In the course of anti-malerial work, quinine was administered to 606 adults out of a total population of 3,540. The incidence of malerial fever is shown below. Discuss the preventive value of quinine.

| | Fever | No fever | Total |
|---|---|---|---|
| Quinine | 19 | 587 | 606 |
| No quinine | 193 | 2741 | 2934 |
| Total | 212 | 3328 | 3540 |

(M.com. Aligarh, 1960) $[X^2 = 10.6 ; x^2_{0.05}$ for v = 1 k 3.841 Quinine is preventive]

6. An experiment was conducted to test the efficacy of chloromycin in checking typhoid. In a certain hospital chloromycin was given to 300 out

400 patients suffering from typhoid. The number of typhoid cases is as follows.

|  | Typhoid | No typhoid | Total |
|---|---|---|---|
| Chloromycin | 40 | 260 | 300 |
| No chloromycin | 60 | 40 | 100 |
| Total | 100 | 300 | 400 |

With the help of $x^2$, test the effectiveness of chloromycin in checking typhoid.

[$X^2 = 87.1$ ; $x^2_{0.05}$ for $v = 1$ k 3.841 chloromycin is effective in checking typhoid]

7.     The following information was obtained in a sample of 50 small general shops.

|  | Shops in towns | Shops in Villages | Total |
|---|---|---|---|
| Run by men | 17 | 18 | 35 |
| Run by Women | 3 | 12 | 15 |
| Total | 20 | 30 | 50 |

Can it be said that there are relatively more women owners of small general shops in villages than in towns?

(Use $x^2$ – test. The 5% value of $x^2$ for $v = 1$k 3.841)

(M.com.,Meerut,1969) [$x^2 = 3.57$ Hypothesis holds good]

8.     A certain drug is claimed to be effective in curing colds.Half of them were given sugar pills. The patients reactions to the treatment are recorded in the following table.

|  | Helped | Harmed | No effect |
|---|---|---|---|
| Drug | 52 | 10 | 18 |
| Sugar pills | 44 | 10 | 26 |

Test the hypothesis that the drug is no better than the sugar pills for curing colds. (The 5% value of $x^2$ for $v = 2 = 5.991$)

9.   You are given the following data. Use $X^2$ test and discuss their significance.

| Boys Father | Intelligent boy | Unintelligent boy | Total |
|---|---|---|---|
| Skilled | 24 | 12 | 36 |
| Unskilled | 32 | 32 | 64 |
| total | 56 | 44 | 100 |

(M.com., Calcutta, 1969) [$x^2 = 2.81$ ; for $v = 1$, $x^2_{0.05} = 3.84$]

10.   In a recent diet survey, the following results were found in a city:

| | Community A | Community B |
|---|---|---|
| Number of families consuming tea | 1236 | 164 |
| Number of families not consuming tea | 564 | 36 |

Discuss whether there is any significant difference between the two communities in the matter of tea taking.

(M.A. Ecom., Punjab, 1965) [$x^2 = 15.247$ ; for $v = 1$, $x^2_{0.05} = 3.841$. The difference is significant]

11.   A random sample of 640 persons from a village provided the following information.

| Effect of influenza | New drug administered | New drug not administered | Total |
|---|---|---|---|
| Attacked | 100 | 60 | 160 |
| Not attacked | 200 | 280 | 480 |
| Total | 300 | 340 | 640 |

Test whether the new drug was effective in preventing the attack of influenza.

12. In recent survey relating to 1000 college students, the data showing coffee- drinking (A) and tea- drinking (B) students is as under

| | A | A | Total |
|---|---|---|---|
| B | 180 | 320 | 500 |
| b | 120 | 380 | 500 |
| Total | 300 | 700 | 1000 |

Discuss whether there is any significant difference amongst the students with regard to coffee and tea- drinking.

13. Explain briefly the following test

   a) Chi – square test

   b) Variance Ratio test

14. With reference to the following data relating to 2 samples, carry out the variance ratio test.

Sample I: 11, 19, 23, 27, 15, 25, 21, 28, 11, 17, 13, 20

Sample II: 10, 14, 17, 10, 16, 18, 20, 17, 19, 19

15. The manufacturer of bicycles of 3 different types A, B and C usually sells 90, 80, 70 bicycles per week. To improve the sales certain modifications were made in the 3 types. The demand pattern changes in the following manner: 105, 85, 74. Test the hypothesis that the modification has not improved the sales.

16. A large hospital bought a total of 500 colour television sets during the past year. Three different brands were purchased and repair records were kept for the first year of each sets operation. The data are given below:

| Brand | Number of repairs | | |
|---|---|---|---|
| | 0 | 1 | 2 or more |
| A | 143 | 70 | 37 |
| B | 90 | 67 | 43 |
| C | 17 | 13 | 20 |

Is there a relationship between brand and number of repairs. Use chi-square test

17.    In a survey, data was collected about the choice of a mobile handset brand among the males and females

| Choice of brand | Males | Females | Total |
|---|---|---|---|
| Nokia | 30 | 40 | 70 |
| Samsung | 50 | 20 | 70 |
| LG | 40 | 20 | 60 |
| Total | 120 | 80 | 200 |

Marketers are interested in knowing whether there is any association between choice of handset and gender. Use chi-square test to find this out. Given value of chi-square =5.991 for 2 d.f at 0.05 level of significance.

18.    An ice cream manufacturer is testing new and old flavours of butterscotch. The research was carried out among heavy, moderate, light and non-users of ice cream. Consumption pattern among corporate was observed as follows:

| Type of user | Number of canteens | |
|---|---|---|
| | New flavour | Old flavour |
| Heavy | 38 | 30 |
| Moderate | 50 | 40 |
| Light | 48 | 44 |
| Non user | 64 | 86 |
| Total | 200 | 200 |

a.  State alternate and null hypothesis

b.  Carry out hypothesis testing for a given Chi square value of 7.81 for 3 d.f at 95% level of confidence

c.  Interpret results

# Multivariate Analysis of data

Marketing facts and figures deal with data that is generated by certain variables. When analysis of data is carried out on the basis of a single variable then such an analysis is termed as 'Univeriate Analysis'. For instance the analysis dealing with the average of the prices of a single commodity in 10 cities. When analysis of data between two variables is carried out for finding the association or correlation then such an analysis is called 'Bivariate Analysis'. For instance, the procedure of finding correlation coefficient between age-groups and salary-groups.

Multivariate Analysis relates to the methodology of estimating the value of a dependent variable on the basis of the values of a certain number (more than two) of independent variables. For instance: multiple correlation coefficient and Multiple Regression equations.

**Some Multiplevariate Techniques are:**

1) Multiple correlation & regression

133

2) Analysis of variance (ANOVA)

3) Discriminant Analysis

## Multiple correlations, partial correlation and multiple regressions

If two variables such as price and demand income and expenditure are related, then the nature and extent of such a relationship can be calculated numerically by means of the coefficient of correlation. Similarly, if three variables such as age, weight, blood pressure of a person are related, then the method of finding correlation consists in finding the combined influence of any two variables, on the third. For instance, we can find the influence of age and weight on the blood pressure. This relationship of the combined influence of two variables on the third is numerically calculated by using the method of multiple correlation coefficients.

Suppose $x_2$, $x_2$ and $x_3$ are three related variables, then the multiple correlation coefficient between $x_1$ on the one hand and $x_2$, $x_3$ on the other is expressed as:

$$R_{1.23} = \sqrt{\frac{r_{12}^2 + r_{13}^2 - 2r_{12}r_{13}r_{23}}{1 - r_{23}^2}}$$

By cyclic changes, we can express the coefficients of relationship between $x_2$ and $x_3$, $x_1$ and also between $x_3$ and $x_1$, $x_2$ as:

$$R_{2.31} = \sqrt{\frac{r_{23}^2 + r_{21}^2 - 2r_{23}r_{21}r_{31}}{1 - r_{31}^2}}$$

And

$$R_{3.12} = \sqrt{\frac{r_{31}^2 + r_{32}^2 - 2r_{31}r_{32}r_{12}}{1 - r_{12}^2}}$$

Here $r_{12}$, $r_{13}$, $r_{23}$ are the respective simple correlation coefficient between $x_1$, $x_2$,; $x_1$, $x_3$ respectively. They are also called zero order coefficients further $r_{12} = r_{21}$, $r_{13} = r_{31}$ and $r_{23} = r_{32}$.

## Problem 1:

Calculate the three multiple correlation coefficients for the following data:

| $X_1$ | 23 | 19 | 17 | 31 | 43 | 27 | 52 | 68 | 71 | 39 |
|---|---|---|---|---|---|---|---|---|---|---|
| $X_2$ | 34 | 26 | 58 | 92 | 63 | 77 | 61 | 79 | 15 | 25 |
| $X_3$ | 26 | 43 | 57 | 52 | 62 | 70 | 59 | 31 | 28 | 32 |

Working and solution

| $X_1$ | $x_1$ | $x_{12}$ | $X_2$ | $x_2$ | $x_{22}$ | $X_3$ | $x_3$ | $x_{22}$ | $x_1 x_2$ | $x_2 x_3$ | $x_3 x_1$ |
|---|---|---|---|---|---|---|---|---|---|---|---|
| 23 | - 16 | 256 | 34 | -19 | 361 | 26 | -20 | 400 | 304 | 380 | 320 |
| 19 | -20 | 400 | 26 | -27 | 729 | 43 | -3 | 9 | 540 | 81 | 60 |
| 17 | -22 | 484 | 58 | 5 | 25 | 57 | 11 | 121 | -110 | 55 | -242 |
| 31 | +8 | 64 | 92 | 39 | 1521 | 52 | 6 | 36 | -312 | 234 | -48 |
| 43 | 4 | 16 | 63 | 10 | 100 | 62 | 16 | 256 | 40 | 160 | 64 |
| 27 | -12 | 144 | 77 | 24 | 576 | 70 | 27 | 576 | -288 | 576 | -288 |
| 52 | 13 | 169 | 61 | 8 | 64 | 59 | 13 | 169 | 104 | 104 | 169 |
| 68 | 29 | 841 | 79 | 26 | 676 | 31 | -15 | 225 | 754 | -390 | -435 |
| 71 | 32 | 1024 | 15 | +38 | 1444 | 28 | -18 | 324 | -1216 | 684 | -576 |
| 39 | 0 | 0 | 25 | +28 | 784 | 32 | -14 | 196 | 0 | 392 | 0 |
| 390 | 0 | 3398 | 530 | 0 | 5280 | 460 | 0 | 2312 | -184 | 2276 | -976 |

$\overline{X_1} = \dfrac{390}{10} = 39$, Also $\overline{X_2} = 53$ and $\overline{X_3} = 46$

$r_{12} = \dfrac{\Sigma x_1 x_2}{\sqrt{\Sigma x_1^2 \cdot \Sigma x_3^2}} = -0.0398 - 0.04$ approx.

$r_{23} = \dfrac{\Sigma x_2 x_3}{\sqrt{\Sigma x_2^2 \cdot \Sigma x_3^2}} = -0.597 = 0.60$ approx.

$r_{31} = \dfrac{\Sigma x_3 x_1}{\sqrt{\Sigma x_3^2 \cdot \Sigma x_1^2}} = -0.348 = -0.35$ approx.

$R_{1.23} = \sqrt{\dfrac{r_{12}^2 + r_{13}^2 - 2\, r_{12} r_{13} r_{23}}{1 - r_{23}^2}}$

$$= \sqrt{\frac{(-0.04)^2 + (-0.35)^2 - 2(-0.04)(-0.35)(0.60)}{1 - (0.60)^2}}$$

$$= 0.4094$$

Calculating, similarly, we get

$R_{2.31} = 0.6268$ and $R_{3.12} = 0.6829$

## Partial correlation

If $X_1, X_2$ and $X_3$ are three different variables which are related amongst themselves then the method of finding the correlation between the variables $X_1$ and $X_2$, keeping the influence of $X_3$ apart (as a constant) is said to be 'partial' and hence in such a case the coefficient of correlation between $X_1$ and $X_2$, which is denoted by $R_{12.3}$ is called partial correlation coefficient'. The dot before the subscripts shows that $X_3$ has been kept as a constant. The formula for calculating $r_{12.3}$ is

$$r_{12.3} = \frac{r_{12} - r_{13} \cdot r_{23}}{\sqrt{1 - r_{13}^2} \sqrt{1 - r_{23}^2}}$$

By cyclic changes, we get

$$r_{23.1} = \frac{r_{23} - r_{21} \cdot r_{31}}{\sqrt{1 - r_{21}^2} \sqrt{1 - r_{31}^2}} \text{ and}$$

$$r_{31.2} = \frac{r_{31} - r_{32} \, r_{12}}{\sqrt{1 - r_{32}^2} \sqrt{1 - r_{12}^2}}$$

## Problem 2:

calculate the three partial correlation coefficient $r_{12.3}$, $r_{12.3}$ and $r_{12.3}$ for the data given in problem 1.

**Solution:**

$$r_{12.3} = \frac{r_{12} - r_{13} \cdot r_{23}}{\sqrt{1 - r_{13}^2} \sqrt{1 - r_{23}^2}}$$

$$= \frac{(-0.04) - (-0.35)(0.60)}{\sqrt{1 - (-0.35)^2} \sqrt{1 - (-0.60)^2}}$$

= 0.2268

= 0.23 approx.

Similarly, the values of the other two partial correlation coefficients can be calculated.

Ans. $r_{23.1} = 0.6261 = 0.63$, $r_{3\_.2} = 0.626 = 0.63$

## Multiple Regression

With reference to a scatter diagram in two dimensions, we find the regression equations corresponding two variables $X_1$ and $X_2$ as the regression equation of $X_1$ on $X_2$ and also the regression equation of $X_2$ on $X_1$. Corresponding to these two regression equations we get two regression lines.

In regard to regression involving three variables $X_1$, $X_2$ and $X_3$, we consider regression planes in three dimensional space. Hence regression plane of $X_1$ on $X_2$ and $X_3$ and its equation can be determined.

The regression equation of $X_1$, on $X_2$ and $X_3$ is given by

$$X_1 - \overline{X_1} = \frac{\sigma_1}{\sigma_2} \left[\frac{r_{12} - r_{13} r_{23}}{1 - r_{23}^2}\right] (x_2 - \overline{x_2}) + \frac{\sigma_1}{\sigma_3} \left[\frac{r_{13} - r_{12} r_{23}}{1 - r_{23}^2}\right] (x_3 - \overline{x_3})$$

$$= b_{12.3} (x_2 - \overline{x_2}) + b_{13.2} (x_3 - \overline{x_3})$$

Where $\sigma_1$ = S.D. of $X_1$ series

$\sigma_2$ = S.D. of $X_2$ series

$\sigma_3$ = S.D. of $X_3$ series

And $b_{12.3}$ and $b_{13.2}$ are the partial regression coefficients.

By cyclic changes we can write the equations of the other two regression planes i.e., $X_2$ cn $X_3$ and $X_1$ and $X_3$ on $X_1$ and $X_2$.

## Problem 3:

Find the multiple regression equation of $X_1$ on $X_2$ and $X_3$ for the data given in problem 1

Calculations: The regression equation of $X_1$ on $X_2$ and $X_3$ is

$$X_1 - \overline{X_1} = b_{12.3} (x_2 - \overline{x_2}) + b_{13.2} (x_3 - \overline{x_3})$$

Now,

$$b_{12.3} = \frac{\sigma_1}{\sigma_2} \left( \frac{r_{12} - r_{13} r_{23}}{1 - r_{23}^2} \right)$$

$$= \frac{18.43}{25.06} \left[ \frac{-0.04 - (-0.35)(0.60)}{1 - (0.60)^2} \right] = 0.1952$$

And $b_{13.2} = \frac{\sigma_1}{\sigma_2} \left[ \frac{r_{12} - r_{13} r_{23}}{1 - r_{23}^2} \right] = -0.6170$

$$\sigma_1 = \sqrt{\frac{\Sigma x_1^2}{n}} = \sqrt{\frac{3380}{10}} = 18.43$$

$$\sigma_2 = \sqrt{\frac{\Sigma x_2^2}{n}} = \sqrt{\frac{6280}{10}} = 25.06$$

and $\sigma_3 = \sqrt{\frac{\Sigma x_3^2}{n}} = \sqrt{\frac{2312}{10}} = 15.20$

on simplification the regression equation of $X_1$ on $X_2$ and $X_3$ is $X_1 = 0.195 \ X_2 - 0.617 \ X_3 + 57.1$.

## 2. Analysis of variance (ANOVA) explained in chapter 8.

## 3. Discriminant Analysis

In the process of marketing research it is sometimes necessary to classify persons or objects into certain classes or groups such as purchasers or non–purchasers. The procedure involves the categorization in an appropriate manner so as to discriminate between the individuals in the different groups. Discriminant analysis enables the prediction of an object's possibility or likelihood of relating to a particular group on the basis of a number of independent variables. If we consider the sales of a particular article, pattern–wise or potentiality–wise on basis of grouping of the regions of sales in terms of good or bad potentiality then by the procedure of discriminant analysis we can identify the predictor or independent variables that discriminate amongst the groups.

In the case of a two – group discriminant analysis the following are the different steps:

i.  Frame a discriminant function such as

Y= $mX_1 + nX_2$ where

$X_1$, $X_2$ are the variables representing the two factors. The value of $m$ and $n$ have to be determined by solving the following two normal equations;

$$m\sum(x_1 - \overline{x_1})^2 + n(x_1 - \overline{x_1})(x_2 - \overline{x_2}) = \overline{x_{1_{g_B}}} - \overline{x_{1_{g_A}}}$$

and $m\sum (x_1 - \overline{x_1})(x_2 - \overline{x_2}) + n\sum(x_2 - \overline{x_2})^2 = \overline{x_{2_{g_B}}} - \overline{x_{2_{g_A}}}$

here $g_B$ and $g_A$ are the respective two groups consisting of the classified data, or the basis of futures such as good, bad or like, dislike etc, and $\overline{x_1}$ and $\overline{x_2}$ are the respective means of the groups and by solving the normal equations we obtain the values of m and n and determine the 'Discriminant function'

ii.  Using the discriminant scores we obtain the variability values between the groups and the variability values within the groups *

iii.  Determine the discriminant ratio as

$$\frac{\text{variability between the groups}}{\text{variability within the groups}}$$

iv.  Validate the discriminant function

v.  Carry out the testing.

## Structural Techniques

When a large complex data involving many variables is analysed into certain appropriate groups then such a process is termed as 'Structural multivariate Analysis'. The following are the commonly used multivariate structural techniques.

a)  Cluster analysis

b)  Factor Analysis

c)  Conjoint Analysis

a)  **Cluster Analysis:** When a huge data is classified into smaller groups or sets on the basis of certain characteristics or similarities then all such small groups are called 'Clusters'. Analytical studies relating to such clusters comprise 'Clusters Analysis'.

b) **Factor Analysis:** Information dealing with the inter-relationships between a large number of variables is analysed on the basis of some appropriate 'Factors'

c) **Conjoint Analysis:** It is a multi-thrust, analytical and examining technique that is of much relevance in market research. According to this technique a number of dimensions relating to products and services are studied. Conjoint Analysis is based on the practical assumption that the analysis involving a number of appropriate features relating to products and services can be more valuable and consistent than the study of a select few. For instance in regard to products such as Electric ceiling Fans or Refrigerators, it is necessary to study jointly important features relating to latest technological design, Brand, size, price, colour etc.

## Cluster Analysis and Example

Suppose we consider the expenditures on necessities and luxuries of 10 different (I to X) families belonging to the higher income Group and Middle Income Group. On an average the size of a family is considered as five member. On the basis of the classification of the data relative to expenditure on necessities and luxuries, we get two clusters consisting of families, as shown in the following diagram. These clusters clearly indicate that families that spend more on necessities spend less on luxuries and vice-versa

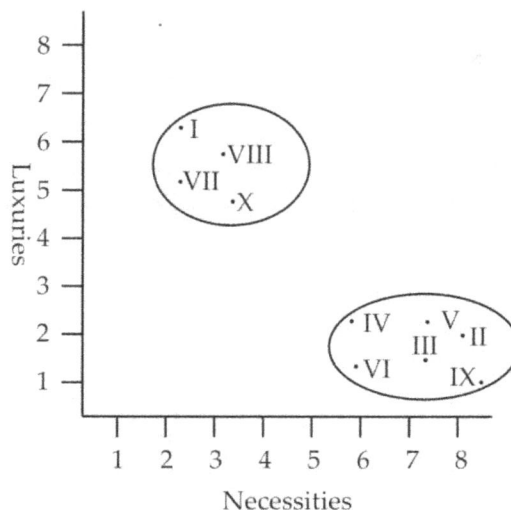

## Factor Analysis: Important features

a) The objective of factor analysis is to group the input variables into minimum number of factors with maximum potentially.

b) Factor analysis which is based on a number of variables determines the factors that show the inter correlations. For instance the attributes of a five– star hotel services and the factor of excellence in service.

c) A researcher in marketing is concerned with the reduction of a mass of data to an appropriate size that is amenable for analysis. This reduction is possible on the basis of identification of the reduced number of factors. Also it is adopted by weighing the variables.

d) The correlation coefficients relating to various pairs of unit variables form a 'correlation coefficient matrix'.

e) Factor loadings: refer to correlation between various combinations of variables and factors. <u>Notation</u> Fi(j) is the factor loading of the variable j on the factor i where

f) $i = 1,2,3, \ldots.n$ and $j = 1,2,3\ldots. n$.

g) The sum of the squares of the factor loadings relating to the variable I on the factors is termed as communality $h_i^2$ when $h_i^2 < \sum_{j=1}^{n} F_{i_j}^2$

h) Eigen Value Corresponding to the factor j is expressed as $\sum_{j=1}^{n} F_{i_j}^2$. If the Eigen Value of a factor is more than or equal to 1 then the factor gets retained, otherwise it is dropped.

## Exercise – IX

Questions:

1.      Explain important multivariate techniques with reference to research studies.

2.      Write an explanatory note on cluster analysis.

3.      What is the importance of multiple discriminant analysis.

4.      Explain the following with suitable illustrations: Univariate, bivariate and multivariate analytical procedures.

5.      Distinguish between univariate and multivariate analysis.

6.      Describe the important aspects of conjoint analysis.

7.      What is factor analysis? Explain briefly.

8.      With reference to the data given below find the 3 multiple regression equations. $\overline{X_1} = 43$, $\overline{X_2} = 48$, $\overline{X_3} = 44$

$r_{12} = -0.27$, $r_{23} = -0.36$, $r_{31} = 0.16$

Ans.    $X_1 = 0.043$, $X_3 - 0.143$ $X_2 + 47.97$

$X_2 = -0.324$ $X_3 - 0.367 X_1 + 78.03$

$X_3 = 0.1145$ $X_1 - 0.34$ $X_2 + 55.4$

9.      Given $R_{12} = 0.3$, $R_{23} = 0.61$ and $r_{31} = 0.24$, calculate $R_{1.23}$, $R_{2.31}$ and $R_{3.12}$

Ans.    $R_{1.23} = 0.39$, $R_{2.31} = 0.66$, $R_{3.12} = 0.61$

10.     Find the multiple and partial correlation coefficients for the following data.

| X | 19 | 21 | 24 | 26 | 27 | 27 | 29 | 31 | 30 | 31 |
|---|----|----|----|----|----|----|----|----|----|----|
| Y | 24 | 28 | 29 | 39 | 30 | 31 | 34 | 35 | 36 | 37 |
| Z | 21 | 2 – | 26 | 30 | 27 | 32 | 31 | 36 | 33 | 38 |

11.  Find the multiple regression equation of $X_1$ on $X_2$ and $X_3$ for the data in Example 10.

12.  Find the multiple correlation $R_{1.23}$, the partial correlation coefficient $R_{23.1}$ and the multiple regression equation of $X_2$ on $X_3$, $X_1$.

| $X_1$ | 55 | 59 | 63 | 68 | 56 | 73 | 82 | 76 | 64 | 74 |
|------|----|----|----|----|----|----|----|----|----|----|
| $Y_1$ | 58 | 60 | 53 | 52 | 61 | 70 | 76 | 77 | 63 | 80 |
| $Z_1$ | 63 | 55 | 51 | 56 | 59 | 74 | 74 | 81 | 61 | 84 |

13.  Find the three multiple correlation coefficients for the following data.

| $X_1$ | 7 | 2 | 6 | 8 | 3 | 5 | 9 | 10 | 15 | 12 |
|------|---|---|---|---|---|---|---|----|----|----|
| $X_2$ | 1 | 5 | 8 | 4 | 9 | 3 | 6 | 7 | 13 | 10 |
| $X_3$ | 3 | 4 | 9 | 2 | 1 | 7 | 5 | 8 | 10 | 14 |

Ans.  $R_{1.23} = 0.68$, $R_{2.31} = 0.61$, $R_{3.12} = 0.695$

14.  Find the multiple regression equation of $X_1$ on $X_2$, $X_3$ for the data given in Example 12.

15.  Find the regression equation of $X_2$ on $X_3$, $X_1$ for the following data.

| $X_1$ | 12 | 16 | 19 | 27 | 29 | 32 | 33 | 39 | 40 | 43 |
|------|----|----|----|----|----|----|----|----|----|----|
| $X_2$ | 7 | 9 | 11 | 13 | 16 | 19 | 24 | 31 | 33 | 37 |
| $X_3$ | 3 | 6 | 9 | 11 | 15 | 21 | 25 | 26 | 34 | 40 |

16.  Calculate the partial regression coefficients $b_{12.3}$ and $b_{13.2}$ for the data in Example 13.

17.  What are the values of the partial correlation coefficients $r_{12.3}$, $r_{23.1}$ and $r_{31.2}$ for the data in example 13.

# Decision Making

Decision making is an essential aspect not only in day to day dealing with human activities but also in the sphere of managerial activities.

While appropriate decisions are beneficial and profitable, unthoughtful and erroneous decisions lead to loss, misery and disaster. Therefore right efforts in meaningful proportions on the basis of timely decisions will always result in an organization's effective operational functioning, productivity and growth.

Decision making involving a problem necessitates a full analysis of the problem on the basis of questions beginning with What? Where? When? How? and so on. Each effect has to be judged in detail so as to decide properly. It should be ensured that the course of action taken on the basis of a decision is consistent with the policies, objectives, goals and as well as the overall development and growth of the organization. Decision makers like the trustees are involved in carrying heavy responsibility as regard to the consequences that follow the implementation of their decisions. In simple terms decision making is a process of selecting the most appropriate alternative among a number of available alternatives. Further, when a number of decisions are to be taken it is necessary to prioritize them so that a proper sequence can be worked out.

## Kinds of decisions

There are two types of decision viz (i) tactical decisions and (ii) strategic decision

Tactical decisions are related to short term decisions such as those pertaining to temporary assignment of certain tasks to certain workers etc. Strategic decisions are long term decisions as they involve greater involvement and commitment of persons, resources, equipment etc. for instance, decision with regard to marketing and launching of a novel product or entering into new areas of product distribution etc.

In the decision making process statistical procedures on the basis of qualitative aspects of outcomes are applied. The probabilities associated with various outcomes are estimated. The outcomes are expressed in the form of monetary payoffs. Inspite of the application of statistical procedures, one cannot deny the importance of judgement or in some cases intuition.

## Decision Criteria

For the various courses of action (alternatives), it is necessary to find the value of each alternative before finalizing the decision. The criteria may be maximization of profit, minimization of cost etc. The value( or worth) of each outcome in terms of profits, sales costs etc; expressed in rupees is called payoff value.

Further qualitative aspects of the products also arise while expressing the value. The outcomes of decision making are always conditioned by environment of certainty or uncertainty. Accordingly decision making is classified as…

   i.    Under certainty (due to deterministic environment)

   ii.    Under risk (due to probabilistic environment)

   iii.   Under uncertainty

## 1.    Under certainty

Decision making under uncertainty arises when the various outcomes of the different courses of action can be predetermined. Hence this process is easily dependable. The outcomes are based on simple calculations involving two or three unknowns and their simultaneous equations or in some cases, simple equations. The following is an example of decision making under certainty.

## Problem – 1

A company can manufacture two different product k1 and k2. The two products have to be processed through two machines m1 and m2 whose available capacity in terms of hours per month are 480 and 410 respectively. Product k1 needs 3 hours of m1 and 1 hour of m2 product k2 requires 1 hour of m1 and 2 hours of m2. Find the number of units of products k1 and k2 to be manufactured every month by utilizing fully the available capacity of the machines.

| Machines | Product time availability | | |
|----------|------|------|------|
| M1 | 3 | 1 | 480 |
| M2 | 1 | 2 | 410 |

This is based on deterministic situation as it is possible to determine as to how many units of product k1 and k2 can be manufactured by fully utilizing the available machine hours capacities of m1 and m2.

**Solution:**

Let x be the number of units of k1 and y be the number of units of k2 that can be manufactured. Then as per the given data we have the following simultaneous equations:

$3x+y = 480$

$X +2y=410$

Solving , we get x=110, y=150

Therefore 110 units of product k1 and 150 units of product k2 can be manufactured.

## i.     Under risk

In business, situations are often unpredictable and involves considerable risk. Hence decision making is subject to risk, and as such the element of probability prevails. In such cases with reasonable estimates of probability the outcomes are calculated.

If for different strategies S1, S2,S3…

$p_1(x_1), p_2(x_2), p_3(x_3),$…………… $p_n(x_n)$ are the respective probabilities associated with events

$E_1, E_2, E_3,$ …………… $E_n$, then the expected monetary value for each strategy (called EMV) is calculated as

EMV = $\sum x j. p(xj)$

Where xj is the payoff with probability p (xj)

The following is an example.

## Problem – 2

For the data given below, calculate expected value under risk.

Events (states of nature)

| Strategies | E1 | E2 | E3 | E4 |
|---|---|---|---|---|
| | 0.15 | 0.25 | 0.40 | 0.20 |
| S1 | 12 | 18 | 24 | −20 |
| S2 | 36 | 16 | 26 | 15 |
| S3 | 15 | 25 | 14 | −22 |
| S4 | 21 | 11 | 10 | 28 |

* Figures against strategies are in lakhs of Rupees.

**Solutions:**

We calculate the expected value of the best strategy based on the highest EMV(Expected Value under Risk)

EMV (S1)      = 12(0.15) + 18(0.25) + 24(0.40) – 20(0.20)

$= 1.8 + 4.5 + 9.6 - 4.0$

$= 11.9$

EMV (S2)    $= 36(0.15) + 16(0.25) + 26(0.40) + 15(0.20)$

$= 5.4 + 4.0 + 10.4 + 3.0$

$= 22.8$

EMV (S3)    $= 15(0.15) + 25(0.25) + 14(0.40) - 22(0.20)$

$= 2.25 + 6.25 + 5.6 - 4.4$

$= 9.70$

EMV (S4)    $= 21(0.15) + 11(0.25) + 10(0.40) + 28(0.20)$

$= 3.15 + 2.75 + 4.0 + 5.6$

$= 15.50$

Here, the best strategy is the one that yields an EMV of 22.8. The best strategy is S2.

## Problem – 3

For the data in problem–2 calculate the following:

1. Expected value under certainty or expected value with perfect information.

2. Value of perfect information.

Solution:

1. Expected value under certainty is calculated as

   Best pay x probability of E1 for E1

   + Best pay of x probability of E2 for E2

   + Best pay of x probability of E3 for E3

   + Best pay of x probability of E4 for E4

   i.e. $36(0.15) + 25(0.25) + 26(0.40) + 28(0.20)$

= 5.4 + 6.25 + 10.4 + 5.6

= 27.65

Therefore, expected value with perfect information = 27.65

i.e. E.V under certainty

2.  Value of perfect information.

= Expected value under certainty – Expected value under risk

= 27.65 – 22.80 = 4.85 lakhs.

## ii. Under uncertainty

There are situations in business where it is not possible to estimate the probabilities for the different events or the states of nature. Irrespective of the strategies, there exists no way for calculation of the expected payoff in an environment where no competition from competitors exist and if a decision in regards to launching of a novel product is to be taken, then the decision criteria will depend on the manufacturers policy and discretion based on experience.

The criteria for decision making under uncertainty are based on the following:

1. Maximin criterion
2. Minimax criterion
3. Maximax criterion
4. Laplace criterion
5. Hurwicz alpha criterion
6. Regret criterion

These criteria are explained with reference to the following problem.

## Problem – 4

Manufacturer of a new detergent powder consisting of three varieties viz. super, fine and glow has decide the appropriate variety of detergent to be launched on the basis of the following estimated payoff according to sales levels.

| Detergent variety | Estimated levels of sales (Units) | | |
|---|---|---|---|
| | 50000 | 25000 | 15000 |
| Super | 45 | 30 | 20 |
| Fine | 60 | 45 | 15 |
| Glow | 75 | 50 | 10 |

## Maximin Criterion

The approach of the decision maker is based on question and pessimism. His strategy is to look for the best outcome from amongst the worst outcome.

In the above problem the minimum payoffs correspond to sales of 15,000 units for the three varieties. The maximum among the three minimum payoffs correspond to the payoff 20, for sales of 15,000 units. Thus by launching the detergent of the first variety super, the decision maker maximizes the minimum payoffs. Hence the strategy is to launch 'super'

## Minimax criterion

Here, the decision-makers attitude is one of optimism. The strategy is to look for the minimum outcome from amongst the maximum outcomes (row wise). Find that the maximum payoffs are 45, 60, 75 corresponding to the sales of 50,000 units. The minimum payoff amongst these is 45, which becomes the strategy to be adopted. Hence the decision maker by launching the detergent of the first variety that is 'super', minimises the maximum payoffs.

| Detergent variety | Estimated levels of sales (units) | | | | Maximin | Minimax |
|---|---|---|---|---|---|---|
| | 50000 | 25000 | 15000 | Min | Max | Minimax |
| Super | 45 | 30 | 20 | 20 | 45 | 45 |
| Fine | 60 | 45 | 15 | 15 | | 60 |
| Glow | 75 | 50 | 10 | 10 | | 75 |

## Maximax criterion

If the decision maker is very much optimistic, then with a high degree of optimism he selects the strategy that gives him the maximum payoff amongst all the maximum payoffs. That is, amongst the maximum payoffs 45, 60, 75 corresponding to the sales of 50,000 units, he selects the payoff 75. Hence his strategy would be to launch the detergent variety 'glow'.

## Laplace criterion

According to this criterion each strategy is assigned the same equal probability. Therefore, for each of the three varieties of detergent the probability is given. The working is as follows:

| Detergent variety | Probability | Estimated levels of sales (units) | | | Expected payoffs |
|---|---|---|---|---|---|
| | | 50000 | 25000 | 15000 | |
| Super | 1/3 | 45 | 30 | 20 | 1/3(45)+1/3(30)+1/3(20)=95/3 |
| Fine | 1/3 | 60 | 45 | 15 | 1/3(60)+1/3(45)+1/3(15)=120/3 |
| Glow | 1/3 | 75 | 50 | 10 | 1/3(75)+1/3(50)+1/3(10)=135/3 |

On comparing the expected payoffs, we find that the maximum payoff is 135/3. This corresponds to the variety 'glow'. Hence the strategy would be to launch the detergent variety 'glow'.

## Hurwicz Alpha Criterion

We have seen earlier that the most pessimistic and most optimistic criteria are the maximin and maximax respectively; which are the two ends on the scale of selection of strategies for the decision maker. Therefore it would be realistic to select an appropriate combination of the two criteria. This criterion of combination has been given by Hurwicz. Here optimism between extreme pessimism (0) and extreme optimism (1) is represented by $\alpha$ which varies between 0 and 1

A decision index (Di) is defined as

$Di = \alpha(Mi) + (1-\alpha)$ mi, where

Mi is the maximum payoff corresponding to $i^{th}$ strategy and mi is the minimum payoff corresponding to the $i^{th}$ strategy.

The value of $\alpha$ depends upon the judgement of the decision maker in accordance with his degree of optimism.

Using the data in the example, we suppose the value of $\alpha$ as 0.55. The various values of decision indices would be:

$D1 = 0.55 (45) + (1-0.55) 20 \quad = 24.75 + 9 \quad = 33.75$

$D2 = 0.55 (60) + (1-0.55) 15 \quad = 33 + 6.75 \quad = 39.75$

$D3 = 0.55 (75) + (1-0.55) 10 \quad = 41.25 + 4.50 = 45.75$

Here the maximum value of D3 corresponds to the strategy of selecting detergent glow. Hence, glow could be launched.

## Regret criterion

When a decision makers select the best payoff corresponding to a strategy then there is no opportunity loss or regret. That is, if you select the strategy to launch variety 'super' corresponding to maximum 20, underestimated level of sales of 15,000 units, then the regret opportunity loss would be 20-20 = 0. But if the decision maker realises later on that he could as well have sale of 50000 units corresponding to the variety 'super' then his opportunity loss or regret would be 45 – 20 = 25. With regard to a sale of 25,000 units for the same strategy, his regret will be 30 – 20 = 10. Hence the regret table would be

| Detergent variety | Estimated levels of sales (units) | | |
|---|---|---|---|
| | 50000 | 25000 | 15000 |
| Super | 25 | 10 | 0 |
| Fine | 45 | 30 | 0 |
| Glow | 65 | 40 | 0 |

Here the maximum regret for each strategy would be the payoffs 25, 45 and 65 respectively. The minimum amongst these is 25 and hence the choice of strategy would correspond to the launching of detergent 'super'.

The following is a comparative table showing the various criteria and corresponding decisions.

| Criterion | Strategy decision (variety of detergent) |
|---|---|
| Maximin | Super |
| Minimax | Super |

| Maximax | Glow |
|---|---|
| Laplace | Glow |
| Hurwicz Alpha | Glow |
| Regret | super |

Comparison of the various criteria indicates that the decision maker may launch 'super' or 'glow'. However, the appropriate decisions depend on the judgement of decision makers. The accuracy of the decision is dependent on the probability estimates. If the probability estimates are reliable than perfection in decision making is assured.

## Decision trees

In the process of decision making a manufacturer or production manager has to consider a number of alternatives and their uncertainties. While analyzing the choices he has to identify the time sequence, according to which various actions and events follow. Each different choice would imply different payoff. This type of analytical process can be represented by a graph in the form of a tree and its branches. Each branch corresponds to an outcome as a result of selection of an alternative (decision).

## Problem – 5

A dealer in costly medical equipment has two choices before him. If he stocks equipment E1 and sells it successfully, he can earn a profit of 80,000. If his deal is a failure he incurres a loss of rupees 2,00,000. On the other hand if he stocks equipment E2 and sells it successfully he can make a profit of rupees 1,20,000, but if he fails his loss would be rupees 1,00,000. With regard to the success of E1 the probability is 0.90 and for the success of E2 the probability is 0.70. How should we decide?

Explain by drawing a tree diagram..

## Solution:

+

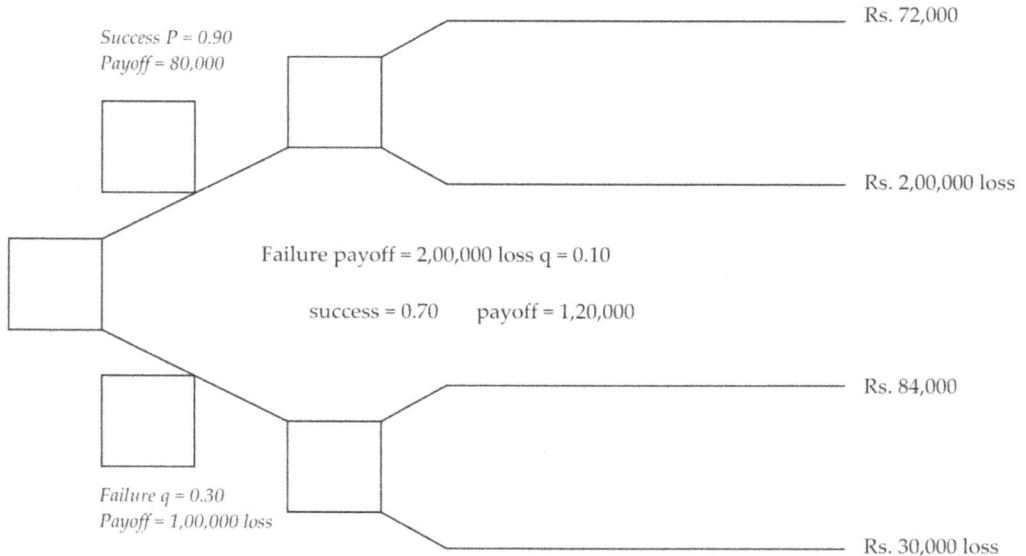

Success P = 0.90
Payoff = 80,000

Rs. 72,000

Rs. 2,00,000 loss

Failure payoff = 2,00,000 loss q = 0.10

success = 0.70    payoff = 1,20,000

Rs. 84,000

Failure q = 0.30
Payoff = 1,00,000 loss

Rs. 30,000 loss

As the EMV in respect of equipment E2 is greater than that of equipment E1 the dealer can decide to stock equipment E2 only.

## Exercise – x

1.  An investor is given the following investment alternatives and percentage rate of return.

| | States of markets (market condition) | | |
|---|---|---|---|
| | Low | Medium | High |
| Regular shares | 2% | 5% | 8% |
| Risky shares | –5% | 7% | 15% |
| Property | –10% | 10% | 20% |

Over the past 300 days, 150days have seen medium market conditions and 60 days had high market increases.

On the basis of these data, state the optimal investment strategy for the investor.

2.     Explain and illustrate the following principles of decision making.

 i.     Laplace

 ii.    Maximin

 iii.   Maximax

 iv.    Hurwicz

 v.     Regret

 vi.    Minimax

3.     Western Thermal Power company is interested in taking loans from banks for their thermal project A, B, C, D and E. The offers of different banks are given below.

| Banks | Interest Rate % | | | | | Maximum credit (in Rs Thousands) |
|---|---|---|---|---|---|---|
| | A | B | C | D | E | |
| Co-operative bank | 15 | 15 | 15 | 13 | 14 | 250 |
| Nationalized bank | 16 | 16 | 16 | 15 | 16 | 400 |
| Private bank | 20 | 18 | 18 | 17 | 17 | Any amount |
| Amount required (in Rs Thousands) | 200 | 150 | 200 | 125 | 75 | |

Considering the different rates of interest, advise Western Thermal Power company, how much loan should be taken from each bank so that the total interest is minimum.

4.     A. What is understood by decision theory? Describe the situations in which decisions are taken:

 i.     With certainty

 ii.    With uncertainty

 iii.   Under risk

       B. What are decision trees? Give application when decision trees are useful.

5.    Payoffs of 3 acts X, Y, Z and the states of nature of L, M, N are given below:

| State of nature | Acts | | |
|---|---|---|---|
| | X | Y | Z |
| L | −20 | −50 | 200 |
| M | 200 | −100 | −50 |
| N | 400 | 600 | 300 |

The probabilities of the state of nature are 0.3, 0.4 and 0.3 respectively. Calculate the EMV for the above data and select the best act.

6.    A. "Quantitative techniques have a scientific approach to complex problems involving decision making". Comment

B. Describe the steps involved in the process of decision making.

7.    A. What techniques are used to solve the problems of decision making under certainty, risk and uncertainty? Discuss them briefly

B. Suresh finds the probability of demand distribution of a luxury car 'S' as follows

| Probability of demand | 0.2 | 0.4 | 0.1 | 0.3 |
|---|---|---|---|---|
| Demand of car each day | 1 | 2 | 3 | 4 |

The selling price of a car Rs. 10,00,000 and it costs to Suresh Rs. 6,00,000. Suresh has always followed a rule for initial purchase–Purchase 3

Find the expected daily profit under the decision rule of buying 3 each morning.

If fees for perfect information is Rs. 1,00,000, calculate expected monetary value of the venture with perfect information EMVPI

8.    A businessman has 2 independent investments A and B available to him, but he lacks the capital to undertake both of them simultaneously. He can choose to take A first and then stop, or if A is successful then take B, or vise versa. The probability of success on A is 0.7, while for B it is 0.4 both investment require an initial capital outlay of Rs. 2000, and both return

nothing if the venture is unsuccessful. Successful completion of A will return Rs. 3000(over cost), while successful completion of B will return Rs. 5000 (over cost). Draw the decision tree and determine the best strategy.

9.  A. explain the meaning of statistical decision theory.

B. A toy company is bringing out a new type of toy. The company is attempting to bring out a full, partial or minimal product line. The company has 3 levels of product acceptance. The management will make a decision on the basis of maximizing expected profit. The data on the 1st year profit (in Rs. Thousands) is given below.

| Product acceptance | Probability | Product line | | |
|---|---|---|---|---|
| | | Full | Partial | Minimum |
| Good | 0.2 | 80 | 70 | 50 |
| Fair | 0.4 | 50 | 45 | 40 |
| Poor | 0.4 | −25 | −10 | 0 |

i.  What is the optimum product line?

ii.  Prepare a table for opportunity losses and find E.O.L

10.  A. what are decision trees? How and in what type of situations are they employed for decision making?

B.  A television dealer finds that the cost of holding a television in stock for a week is Rs. 50. Customers who cannot obtain new televisions immediately tent to go to other dealers and he estimates that for every customer who cannot get immediate delivery, he loses an average of Rs. 250. For 1 particular model of television, the probabilities of a demand of 0,1,2,3,4 and 5 televisions in a week are 0.05, 0.10, 0.20, 0.35, 0.25 and 0.05 respectively. How many televisions per week should the dealer order? (Assume that there is no time lag between ordering and delivery) Also find EMVPI.

# Marketing Research Report Writing

## Introduction

Marketing research is related to a specific market problem where there is collection of facts relating to the marketing of a company's product or service. It is possible to obtain the required information on the basis of an appropriate survey that is carried out systematically. In particular the purpose of the survey research is twofold

i)      The assessment of the concerned market and the location of the problem related customers, the specific number of consumers for the concerned product, the nature of the market size and details relating to the distribution activities and strategies adopted for selling. Further the effectiveness of the sales is assessed and the trend of the promotional activities is charted.

ii)   Product evaluation is an important feature of research study. The study relates to the assessment of the consumers' requirements, their attitude regarding the product and their preferences with regards to the price.

In recent times, marketing intelligence is an essential part of every survey activity relating to various products. The main reason for the necessity of awareness in regard to this type of marketing intelligence is to judge the competitive advantage that a manufacturer has. Information relating to the under mentioned categories of marketing research is necessary for assessment of appropriate marketing intelligence.

a)   Product research

b)   Market Segmentation

c)   Distribution research

e)   Advertisement research

## Research report

When a survey is carried out with reference to a particular product or service ,much relevant information is collected, classified , analysed and interpreted for the purpose of enabling the market department or the concerned top management of the manufacturing company to take appropriate action and decisions. For  this purpose the market surveyor or researcher has to present the facts and figures in an appropriate manner in the form of a report. Therefore a market research report is a complete presentations from A to Z of all the collected facts and figures, analysis and interpretations along with the necessary enclosures or appendices. The main objective of the report is to help decision making with respect to marketing problems. If the research work is his own original work that has been carried out, as a result of his enthusiastic interest, then, it has to be publicised effectively so that his findings could be critically scrutinized by the concerned experts. The positive benefit and the worth of the research would be lost if it does not see the light of the day. A researcher has to effectively communicate his research findings to all the interested individuals, expert groups or research organisations through an appropriate research report.

## Various types of research reports

i)      Information reports

ii)     Application reports

iii)    Technical reports

iv)     Decision oriented report

### i)    Information reports

Information reports are basically prepared for the purpose of providing some news or views or opinions of a person or a researcher for the use of the concerned persons. Also the reports of researchers are basically aids or preliminary drafts that serve as basis in preparing advanced or final reports.

### ii)    Publication reports

Publication reports consists of various articles based on earlier researches. Also these publications consists of business or market research articles published in trade journals ,professional journals and also in certain bulletins.

### iii)    Technical reports

These are basically concerned with scientific and technical facts and figures along with the relevant appendices to help a researcher in carrying out his research on the basis of further reference.

### iv)    Decision oriented reports

These reports are of much relevance to the marketing department as they provide useful guidelines to the decision makers or the directors of the companies or the chief executives in regard to the adoption of important policies and marketing programs. Also sales promotional activities can be carried out in accordance with the timely decisions of the executives.

## Essentials of report writing (in general)

Report writing is essentially based on a research investigation. The information has to be put in appropriate use by the concerned person. For this reason it is necessary to adhere to the following principles :

a)      the main objective of the research presentation has to be noted carefully.

b)      type of research person or persons for whom the research findings are meant should be noted.

c)      The details in the report should be presented clearly keeping in mind the essential parts of a research report as explained below:

Research report consists of the following three essential parts (format of a report)

**Part I:**   Preliminary part

**Part II:**   Substance of the research

**Part III:**   Appendices

## Explanation of part I

The preliminary part should consist of the following pages

1.      Title page

2.      Preface and acknowledgements

3.      List of tables

4.      List of graphs and diagrams

5.      Contents (chapter wise)

The title should be simple, clear and appropriately worded so as to be self explanatory. It should not be too lengthy and ambiguous. It should be attractive and interesting so as to attract the attention of a learned observer. The preface should carry briefly the message of the researcher, along with due acknowledgements that sincerely express thankfulness of the researcher to all those responsible for the successful completion of the research. The list of tables should be provided in a sequential form. The page number pertaining to each table should be mentioned for quick reference. List of graphs and diagrams should be provided, in accordance with the sequence of chapters. The contents page should contain the chapter heading in a proper order.

## Explanation of part II

This is the most important part of the research report as it contains the total substance (text) of the research. The following in general should be the sequence of the chapters

## Chapter I: Introduction

This chapter should provide the introductory details relating to the problem of research. Contain the background information, stating the facts, happenings and observations that enthused or promoted the researcher to undertake the investigative study. The topic of research should be meaningfully introduced.

## Chapter II: Survey of literature

Research on various topics in the areas of business commerce and social sciences is generally based on an extensive study carried out by a researcher. In regard to the topic of study appropriate sources of information should be sought by visiting various libraries and research institutions. Study tours, for details observation and on the spot survey should be undertaken.

Literature survey is a matter of painstaking efforts and persistent searching, vision of the researcher. Much time, money and energy would be required in tracing as wide and extensive literature as possible. Literature survey is the backbone of research.

## Chapter III: Objectives, hypothesis and methodology

A research should clearly spell out the necessary objectives of research. The objective should be pertinent to the problem of research. The number of objectives should not be very large. Each objective should be precisely worded. Hypothesis should be relevantly framed so as to be consonance with the objectives. Hypothesis should not be too many as that would lead a researcher astray from his searching goal.

Depending upon the nature of the problem, area and type of research, methodology should be designed. The researcher should substantiate his sampling methodology.

## Chapter IV: Collection of data

This chapter should provide various details relating to methods of collecting primary data. Sources of secondary data should be stated. Details of the questionnaire and schedules used should be explained. Precautions taken by the researcher to maintain accuracy and minimise the errors, if any, should be stated. The collected data should be presented in a properly classified and tabulated manner.

## Chapter V: Analysis of data

The research report should carefully specify the tools and techniques that were used in the analysis of data. In the course of analysis appropriate statistical techniques should be used to validate the hypothesis.

## Chapter VI: Findings, interpretations and conclusions

This chapter contains the essence of research. Analysis leads to findings that necessitate logical interpretation. A researcher can objectively state his conclusions.

## Chapter VII: Suggestions and recommendations

Research investigations and in-depth studies provide new knowledge and experience to a researcher. This in turn would require a researcher to have a degree of expertise and insight, so as to enable him to suggest some guidelines to all those interested. Further, a researcher gains a measure of confidence and certainity in his research findings, so as to make recommendations.

## Part III: Appendices

To provide an adequate support to the substance in part II, a researcher may provide additional details for the purpose of reference. These are called appendices or enclosures. For instance, bibliography and questionnaires are used. These are quite helpful as supportive reference material. However, the number of appendices should not be too large.

## Exercise XI

### Questions :

1.    Describe briefly the layout of a research report

2.    Explain the importance of a marketing research report

3.    Explain the sequence of steps involved in a marketing research report.

4.    What are the essentials of a good research report.

5.    What precautions you would take in preparing a marketing research report?

6.    Write explanatory notes on the following:
      a) Importance of findings and interpretations
      b) Usefulness of bibliography in research report
      c) Characteristics of a good research report
      d) Appendices for a good research report

7.    Describe briefly the various types of research reports

# Additional Exercises

---

**Exercise (I)**

---

i.   Fill in the blanks with the appropriate word.

1.   Research is an objective oriented _____ study.
     a) Proper
     b) Analytical
     c) Dependent
     d) Independent

2.   While selecting the topic of research it is necessary to consider the _____ of the topic.
     a) Significance
     b) Rationale
     c) Relevance
     d) Usefulness

3. **The main objective of research is to find _____ to questions**
   a) Conclusions
   b) Answers
   c) Solutions
   d) Remedies

4. **Random sampling is essentially based on _____ sampling.**
   a) Probability
   b) Usual
   c) Appropriate
   d) popular

5. **_____ research is a common feature of modern times.**
   a) Scientific
   b) Social
   c) Inter-disciplinary
   d) Basic

6. **Research problems that are_____ should be avoided.**
   a) Complex
   b) Ambiguous
   c) Worthless
   d) Insignificant

7. **Modern technology has very much accelerated the process of _____ research.**
   a) Investigative
   b) Internet
   c) Marketing
   d) Social

ii. **State whether the following statements are True or False**

8. **Case- study method follows the descriptive approach than the analytical.**
   a) True
   b) False

9. A good research design minimizes experimental errors in an investigation.
   a) True
   b) False

10. Stratified sampling is a non-probability method of sampling.
    a) True
    b) False

## (Ex-1) Answers

| 1(b) | 2(a) | 3(b) | 4(a) | 5(c) | 6(b) | 7(a) | 8(b) | 9(a) | 10(b) |
|------|------|------|------|------|------|------|------|------|-------|

## Exercise (2)

i. State whether the below statements are True or False:

1. A good hypothesis should possess conceptual clarity and precision
   a) True
   b) False

2. Hypothesis testing involves either accepting or rejecting a null hypothesis.
   a) True
   b) False

3. Alternate hypothesis is more important than null hypothesis.
   a) True
   b) False

4. Questionnaire method is not useful in the case of large scale enquiries.
   a) True
   b) False

5. Stratified sampling is probability method of sampling.
   a) True
   b) False

6. Technology evolution is brining information technology to masses.
    a) True
    b) False

III    Tick mark the correct answers

7. Which of the following measures of central tendency is based on 50% of the central values?
    a) Mode
    b) Mean
    c) Median
    d) Both 'a' and 'b'

8. What are the limits of the coefficient of correlation?
    a) 1 and 0
    b) No limits
    c) 1 and +1
    d) 0 and +1

9. 'dispersion' implies
    a) Deviations between items
    b) Scatter amongst a set of items
    c) Both 'a' and 'b'
    d) Neither 'a' nor 'b'

10. The following data shows the daily wages of workers

| Daily wages (in Rs.) | 50–60 | 60–70 | 70–80 | 80–90 | 90–100 |
|---|---|---|---|---|---|
| No of workers | 14 | 22 | 28 | 24 | 12 |

What is the percentage of workers earning Rs 70 and more but less than Rs. 90 as daily wages?
    a) 38%
    b) 52%
    c) 64%
    d) 72%

11. **Authenticity and relevance of a research investigation is based on the assurance of an error-free _____ reliability of the collected data.**
    a) Quantitative
    b) Qualitative
    c) Absolute
    d) Relative

## (Ex-2) Answers

| 1(a) | 2(a) | 3(b) | 4(b) | 5(a) | 6(a) | 7(c) | 8(c) | 9(c) | 10(b) | 11(b) |
|------|------|------|------|------|------|------|------|------|-------|-------|

## Exercise (3)

1. Explain the various stages of research process?

2. What is a research design explain the characteristics of good research design?

3. Explain the importance of scaling techniques and also explain the use of semantic and Likert scales?

4. What is marketing Research? Explain the importance of Marketing Research?

5. What are the various steps you would take in preparing a good marketing research Report?

6. Write short notes on any3 of the following:-

   a. Retail Shop Audit

   b. Test Marketing

   c. TV Audience Research

   d. Sales Promotion Research

   e. Expected Monetary Value

## Exercise (4)

1. What is marketing Research? Explain the aims and objectives of marketing research.

2. Distinguish between 'Research Methods' and 'Research Methodology'

3. A Retail outlet engaged in selling consumer durable suddenly experiences a downfall in the sales. As a manager of the retail outlet design a questionnaire to assess the down fall.

4. Write explanatory notes on any two of the following;

   a. Method of collecting primary data.

   b. Limitations of marketing research.

   c. Methods of probability sampling.

5. A ramdom sample of 400 apples from a large consignment showed 40 apples as rotten. Estimate the parentage of rotten apples in the entire consignment. Find 95% confidence limits for the parentage of rotten apples in the consignment.

6. The data given below shows the performance of 11 students in Business statistics in 2 different tests conducted before providing them with coaching and after 10 weeks of coaching. Find out whether coaching has benefitted the student or not.

| Marks before coaching | 48 | 54 | 65 | 74 | 59 | 23 | 41 | 46 | 65 | 72 | 45 |
|---|---|---|---|---|---|---|---|---|---|---|---|
| Marks after coaching | 54 | 52 | 63 | 79 | 86 | 78 | 34 | 50 | 62 | 86 | 58 |

[Given t =2.23 for 10d.f]

0.05

7. The following table shows the result of inoculation against cholera in a certain village.

| Effects of Cholera | Inoculated | Not Inoculated |
|---|---|---|
| Attacked | 620 | 380 |
| Not Attacked | 550 | 450 |

[given $X^2 = 3.841$ for 1d.f]

0.05

Find out whether inoculation is effective in controlling cholera.

## Exercise (5)

1. What is marketing Research? Explain the aims and objectives of marketing research.

2. Distinguish between 'Research Methods' and 'Research Methodology'

3. A Retail outlet engaged in selling consumer durable suddenly experiences a downfall in the sales. As a manager of the retail outlet design a questionnaire to assess the down fall.

4. Write explanatory notes on any two of the following;

   a. Sources of secondary data.

   b. Limitations of marketing research.

   c. Methods of Non-probability sampling.

5. A ramdom sample of 500 apples from a large consignment showed 50 apples as rotten. Estimate the parentage of rotten apples in the entire consignment. Find 95% confidence limits for the parentage of rotten apples in the consignment.

6. The data given below shows the performance of 11 students in Business statistics in 2 different tests conducted before providing them with coaching and after 10 weeks of coaching. Find out whether coaching has benefitted the student or not.

| Marks before coaching | 50 | 56 | 67 | 76 | 61 | 25 | 43 | 48 | 67 | 74 | 47 |
|---|---|---|---|---|---|---|---|---|---|---|---|
| Marks after coaching | 56 | 54 | 65 | 81 | 88 | 80 | 36 | 52 | 64 | 88 | 60 |

[Given t =2.23 for 10d.f]

0.05

7. The following table shows the result of inoculation against cholera in a certain village.

| Effects of Cholera | Inoculated | Not Inoculated |
|---|---|---|
| Attacked | 720 | 480 |
| Not Attacked | 650 | 550 |

[given X² = 3.841 for 1d.f]

0.05

Find out whether inoculation is effective in controlling cholera.

# Appendices

# Appendix I

# Specimen Questionnaires

## SPECIAL AND EXHAUSTIVE QUESTIONNAIRES

1) An exhaustive questionnaire for the collection of data pertaining to the evaluation of performance of premier nationalised banks and foreign banks in India

## Part A: Bank Performance

N.B Kindly indicate your answer b putting (   ) in the appropriate box

1.  Name of the bank

2.  Location

3.  Officer's Designation

4.  As a basis of promotion   Male [ ]        Female [ ]

5.  Age                 Below 30 years  [ ]

6.  Lenght of service in the banking industry

    Less than 3 years    [ ]

    3 - 5 years          [ ]

    5 – 10 years         [ ]

    10 – 15 years        [ ]

    15 – 20 years        [ ]

    More than 20 years   [ ]

7.  Length of service in this bank

    Less than 3 years    [ ]

3 - 5 years ☐

5 – 10 years ☐

10 – 15 years ☐

15 – 20 years ☐

More than 20 years ☐

8.   Please state the area of your primary responsibility at present

_____

_____

9.   What are the various services offered by your bank.

(a)   Personal Banking/Retail Banking

(b)   Corporate banking

(c)   Overdraft facilities

(d)   ATM banking

(e)   Electronic banking (ECS & EFT)

(f)   Net banking

(g)   Private banking

(h)   Please specify services other than those included above

_____

_____

10.   Which of the following types of loans are offered to individuals by your bank

(a)   Personal loans

(b)   Loans against shares

(c)     Educational loans

(d)     Consumer loans

(e)     Car loans

(f)     Housing loan

(g)     Any other loan please specify

---

11.     How do you compare the overdraft facilities being extended to corporates and individuals with the various loans as mentioned above in terms of

(a)     Interest rate          ☐

(b)     Easy availability     ☐

(c)     Documentation      ☐

(d)     Repayment           ☐

12.     Which of the following types of loans are being offered to the corporates/companies

(a)     Short term deposits /ICD     ☐

(b)     Short term loans     ☐

(c)     Long term loans     ☐

(d)     Leasing/hire purchase     ☐

(e)     Foreign currency loans     ☐

(f)     Infrastructure loans     ☐

(g)     Any other loans please specify

---

13.     Which of the investment facilities are being offered

(a)     Time deposits          ☐

(b)    Fixed deposits    ☐

(c)    Mutual funds    ☐

(d)    Any other please state _____

14.    Retail banking is the new mantra in banking sector .Which product in retail banking forms a major part of your asset portfolio?

(a)    Home loans    ☐

(b)    Consumer loans    ☐

(c)    Car loans    ☐

(d)    Educational loans    ☐

(e)    Any other loan please specify _____

15.    How would you compare fixed deposits with fixed income plans F.D Kisan Vikas Patra, National Saving Certificates, Fixed Income Plans, Public Provident Funds in terms of:

(a)    Interest rate (High/Low)    ☐

(b)    Maturity (Long term/ Short term)    ☐

(c)    Withdrawal (Premature/on maturity)    ☐

(d)    Renewal    ☐

(e)    Documentation procedures (Simplicity)    ☐

(f)    Any other reason,please state_____

16.    With foreign banks/ and privatisation of various banks,which factors/services/areas are getting affected of nationalized banks?

  a)  Factors:    ☐

  b)  Competition    ☐

  c)  Interest rates    ☐

  d)  Documentation    ☐

e) Processing ☐

f) Security on loan ☐

g) Any other please state_____

Services

a) Loans ☐

b) Deposits ☐

c) ATM banking ☐

d) Internet banking ☐

e) E-Banking ☐

f) Phone baking ☐

g) Mobile banking ☐

17. With ATM banking era,is any debit card or credit card facility being offered by your bank?

   Yes ☐          No ☐

18. Does your bank provide depositary services?

   Yes ☐          No ☐

19. As regards, foreign remittances which factors are affecting

| | Strongly agree A | Agree B | Disagree C |
|---|---|---|---|
| Time taken for transfere | ☐ | ☐ | ☐ |
| Documentation Procedure | ☐ | ☐ | ☐ |
| Ceiling on amount | ☐ | ☐ | ☐ |
| Service charges | ☐ | ☐ | ☐ |
| RBI regulations | ☐ | ☐ | ☐ |

Any other please specify_____

20. The concept of private banking does not exist in India. Do you think introducing the same would benefit customers?

    Yes ▢          No ▢

    If yes please state :


    If No why?

21. Phone banking/mobile banking/internet banking is now popular in private and foreign banks. However, the same is not yet functional on large scale in nationalised banks

    Agree ▢          Disagree ▢

22. To what extent is technology management important to your bank in terms of

    |                                   | Full Extent | Some Extent |
    |-----------------------------------|:-----------:|:-----------:|
    | Computerization                   | ▢           | ▢           |
    | Financial systems and applications| ▢           | ▢           |

    Any other please specify_____

23. Electronic fund transfer and Electronic clearing system are playing an important role in today's world of e-banking

    Agree ▢                    Disagree ▢

    Does your bank also provide these facilities to clients?

    Yes ▢                    No ▢

24. Risk management is considered to be the most crucial aspect in banking

    Agree ▢                    Disagree ▢

25. One of the parameters measuring risk is security 'obtained for loans'. Security is taken in the following ways for loans:

|                                  | Strongly Agree<br>A | Agree<br>B |
|----------------------------------|:---:|:---:|
| Security in the form of shares   | ☐ | ☐ |
| a) Promissory note               | ☐ | ☐ |
| b) Deposits                      | ☐ | ☐ |
| c) Property                      | ☐ | ☐ |

d) Any other Kind of security, please mention_____

26. The following variables are considered for evaluation of credit and to avoid N.P.A

|                                     | Strongly Agree<br>A | Agree<br>B |
|-------------------------------------|:---:|:---:|
| a) Analysis of financial statements | ☐ | ☐ |
| b) Obtaining security               | ☐ | ☐ |
| c) Obtaining security               | ☐ | ☐ |
| d) Evaluation of trade/business     | ☐ | ☐ |

e) Any other evaluation, please mention_____

27. What is the approximate percentage of assets that have become N.P.A. as of March 03 of your bank

a) Less than 10% of assets/portfolio  ☐

b) Between 10% - 20% of assets/portfolio  ☐

c) Between 20% - 30%  ☐

d) Above 30%  ☐

28.     Strategy for removing an asset out of NPA

                                                        YES         NO

(a)     Repayment of credit-over delay period and       ☐           ☐
        charge penal interest

(b)     Recover credit by way of property mortgaged if any   ☐       ☐

(c)     Selling shares                                  ☐           ☐

(d)     Withdrawal of fixed deposit                     ☐           ☐

(e)     Filing a legal suit                             ☐           ☐

(f)     Writing off the assets                          ☐           ☐

(g)     Any other method, please state_____

29.     The following are measures to improve banking sector .Please state
        whether you agree or disagree

                                                        Agree       Disagree

Tighter asset classification norms                      ☐           ☐

Lowering exposure to single borrower and                ☐           ☐

group exposure to a particular sector

Higher provisioning norms                               ☐           ☐

Dispensing concept of 'past due' for recognition of NPAs   ☐        ☐

30. How far do you agree with the following demands of today's customers?

| | | Full agree | Doubtful | Disagree | Strongly Disagree |
|---|---|---|---|---|---|
| a) | Safety | ☐ | ☐ | ☐ | ☐ |
| b) | Easy accessibility | ☐ | ☐ | ☐ | ☐ |
| c) | A higher rate on deposits | ☐ | ☐ | ☐ | ☐ |
| d) | A lower rate on deposit | ☐ | ☐ | ☐ | ☐ |
| e) | Convenient | ☐ | ☐ | ☐ | ☐ |
| f) | Prompt and courteous | ☐ | ☐ | ☐ | ☐ |
| g) | Help and advice in times of need | ☐ | ☐ | ☐ | ☐ |
| h) | Modern technological facilities such as phone and net banking | ☐ | ☐ | ☐ | ☐ |
| i) | Prefer a government controlled bank | ☐ | ☐ | ☐ | ☐ |
| j) | Deposit-locker facilities | ☐ | ☐ | ☐ | ☐ |
| k) | A wide variety of loan products | ☐ | ☐ | ☐ | ☐ |
| l) | Smooth transaction between their savings and fixed deposit accounts | ☐ | ☐ | ☐ | ☐ |

31. MIS and computer reports are increasingly and effectively being used by our bank management

    a) Fully agree ☐

    b) Doubtful ☐

    c) Disagree ☐

    d) Strongly disagree ☐

32. What are the improvements brought about computerization in your bank?

Yes No To some Can't say

extent

a) Decreased the cost of operations
b) Improved the speed of operations
c) Improved accuracy of recording keeping
d) Enhance the quality of information
e) Improved the speed of data processing
f) Provided better use of human resources
g) Enabled better use of money in banks
h) Provided better services to customers
i) Improved management decision making
j) Made possible better management control
k) Created new jobs in the organisation
l) Reduced the clerical work load
m) Improved the overall image of the bank

33. Class banking to mass banking has lead to the increase in the incidence of crimes in banks such as frauds, robberies, etc. and also to the deterioration in bank services and efficiency

(a) Yes [ ]     (b) No [ ]     (c) To some extent [ ]     (d) Can't say [ ]

34. Do you believe that both the supervisory and clerical staff in the banks, either independent of external elements or in connivance with outsiders are responsible for bank frauds?

(a) Yes [ ]     (b) No [ ]     (c) To some extent [ ]     (d) Can't say [ ]

35. Do you think that bank frauds arise on account of the failure on the part of the bank staff to follow meticulously rules, instructions and guidelines?

(a) Yes [ ]     (b) No [ ]     (c) To some extent [ ]     (d) Can't say [ ]

36. Do you believe that external elements perpetrate frauds on banks by ingenuous forgeries or manipulations of cheques, drafts, mail, transfers and other instruments?

(a) Yes ☐　　(b) No ☐　　(c) To some extent ☐　　(d) Can't say ☐

37. Do you agree with the following statements? Indicate your answer by putting a tick( ) in the box.

a) We must fortify the banking sector with futuristic technology and multitalented human capital

b) Validate software to be used by the bank

c) "IDRBT should share its experience and expertise with other developing countries"

d) Sensitize banks to global developments

e) Provide more band width and set benchmark for software to be adopted

f) Recommend technological solutions which are intra industry compatible

g) The only way to discover the limits of the possible is to go beyond them into the realm of the impossible

h) The benefit of net banking are evident, besides convenience , cost per transaction are also low, just 10% of traditional banking

i) Technology has not only slashed set up and transaction cost,but also facilitates electronic bill payment systems

j) As customer convenience is the key word banks are contesting with each other to provide new attractive services

38    Banks conduct business through internet to reduce delivery costs

(a) Yes ☐    (b) No ☐    (c) To some extent ☐    (d) Can't say ☐

39.    Banking operations through internet will increase risk of operation in a new environment

(a) Yes ☐    (b) No ☐    (c) To some extent ☐    (d) Can't say ☐

40.    Risks can be reduced through the use of digital signature

(a) Yes ☐    (b) No ☐    (c) To some extent ☐    (d) Can't say ☐

41.    Internet book-keeping and record maintenance through computers ,creates a paperless environment

(a) Yes ☐    (b) No ☐    (c) To some extent ☐    (d) Can't say ☐

42.    A paperless stage has not been reached in our bank

(a) Yes ☐    (b) No ☐    (c) To some extent ☐    (d) Can't say ☐

43.    Electronic fund transfer is gaining momentum. Is it safe in your opinion

(a) Yes ☐    (b) No ☐    (c) To some extent ☐    (d) Can't say ☐

44.    What have been the initiatives in implementing IT in your bank?

(a) Yes ☐    (b) No ☐    (c) To some extent ☐    (d) Can't say ☐

45.    What steps are being taken up on security in form of labour and equipment issues?

46.    What is different about your bank's IT strategy

47.    According to you what should be the role IDRBT in regard to :

a)  R&D
b)  Global interface
c)  Beyond traditional banking
d)  HRD
e)  Rural markets

48. What qualities should a bank manager have? Please tick the relevant answer

   a) Strong leadership ☐

   b) Effectiveness and competence in his job ☐

   c) Ability to develop subordinate responsibility ☐

   d) Open mindedness and willingness to listen ☐

   e) Ability to develop subordinates ☐

   f) Concern for employees ☐

49. What does every bank owe its employees?

   a) Fair pay and basic benefits ☐

   b) Decent working conditions ☐

   c) Feedback on performance ☐

   d) Opportunity for advancement ☐

   e) Job security ☐

   f) A morally sound environment ☐

50. What does every employee owe his or her bank?

   a) A fair days work ☐

   b) Being a team player ☐

   c) Blind allegiance ☐

   d) Other please state ☐

51. According to you what should salary be based on:

   a) Performance ☐

   b) Seniority ☐

c) Loyalty to the company ☐

d) Responsibility ☐

e) Market value ☐

52. Considering your own merits and contributions to the bank, do you think that you are paid:

a) Quite well ☐

b) Just the right amount ☐

c) Too little ☐

d) Can't say ☐

53. What are the various categories of employees in your bank?

a) Clerical staff and computer operator

b) Supervisory staff and officers

c) Managerial staff

d) Trainers

e) MIS/EDP managers

f) Computer auditors

g) Telecommunication experts

h) Ant other_____

54. What according to you are the objectives of performance appraisal systems in banks?

Yes     No     Can't say

As a basis of promotion

a) For proper placement of people

b) Identification of potential and development ofthe employee

c) Career path planning/succession planning

d) Identification or training needs for proper placement of people.

e) Assessing the strengths and weaknesses of staff and helping him/her in overcoming the weaknesses

f) Any other please specify_____

55. What is your opinion about the purpose served by the present performance appraisal system in your bank?

| | Most of the times | Sometimes | Very few times | Never |
|---|---|---|---|---|
| a) Promotion identification of training needs | | | | |
| b) Employee development employees | | | | |
| c) Placement punishment | | | | |
| d) Just a record | | | | |

56. Do you agree with the following statements?

| | Strongly Agree | Agree | Disagree | Strongly Disagree |
|---|---|---|---|---|
| a) We are given full Credit for what we do here | | | | |
| b) A friendly atmosphere prevails among people in this organisation | | | | |
| c) The current appraisal formats give greater weightages to behavioural/personality traits | | | | |
| d) The tendency to pass responsibility to others in common here | | | | |

e) Working as ateam is not very
much seen here

f) There is not enough recognition
given for good work in the
organisation

g) People do not trust each other here

h) The present appraisal formats are
not designed to reflect actual
performance adequately

i) Our superiors provide necessary
help whenever we are in difficulties

j) The performance appraisal should
be made open ie.the appraise should
be made aware of the appraisal by the appraiser

57. Do you agree with the fact that rural banking is helpful to:

|  | Yes | No |
|---|---|---|
| a) Agricultural farmers | ☐ | ☐ |
| b) Small industries and units | ☐ | ☐ |

c) Any other, please specify_____

58. In order to calculate the productivity of bank employees and branches, kindly provide the following information:

a) Number of employees in your
branches_____

b) Approximate total number of employees in all branches

_____

c) Number of branches in Pune and
Mumbai_____

d) Total number of branches all over India _____

59. Kindly let us know the Prime Lending Rate (PIR) of your bank _____

60.  Would you like to suggest any innovative change in products or services for future to enhance customer's satisfaction?

(a) Yes [ ]                               (b) No [ ]

If yes , please state your suggestion:

# Questionnaires on Customer Service

## Part B:customer service

1.    **Name of Bank:**

2.    **Location:**

3.    **Customer Age:**

   a)  Below 20 years

   b)  20-35

   c)  35-50

   d)  50-60

   e)  Above 60 years

4.    **Sex: Male**                    Female

5.    **Occupation**

   a)  Service

   b)  Professional

   c)  Business

   d)  Farmer

   e)  Student

   f)  Household

   g)  Retired

   h)  h. Others

6.    **Income per month**

   a)  Below Rs 10,000 p.m

   b)  Rs10,000  -Rs 25,000 p.m

   c)  Rs 25,000 – Rs 40,000 p.m

   d)  Rs 40,000 – Rs 50,000 p.m

e) e.AboveRs 50, 000 p.m

7.    **For the last how many years are a customer of this bank?**

a)  Less than one year

b)  1 -5 Years

c)  More than 5 years

8.    **Please tick the facilities existing with this bank**

a)  Saving Bank

b)  Current Account

c)  FD

d)  Loans

e)  Any other please state_____

9.    **Please indicate from amongst the following which prompt you to open an account with this bank:**

a)  Conveniently located

b)  Impressed by the image of the bank

c)  Personal contact with some staff member

d)  You friend/relation had an account and he recommended his bank to you

e)  Any other reason please specify

10.   **How long does it generally take -**

a)  To deposit cash in your account and obtain a receipt _____ mts.

b)  To withdraw cash from your account _____mts.

c)  To get anew check book _____mts.

Due to take your passbook to the branch whenever you -

                    Yes                 No

a)  Deposit cash

b)  Withdraw cash

If not, how often do you give your passbook for completing the entries? _____ times a year.

If yes are the entries completed and the passbook returned to you immediately

             Yes           No

If the passbook is not returned immediately, normally after how many days interval are you asked to collect the compeleted passbook _____days.

Do you always get it completed on due date?

    a. Yes       b. No

11.    **Are you able to clearly understand the entries made in your passbook?**
       a. Yes     b. No

If NOT is it due to:
                            Yes           No

Abbreviations used in writing the entries

Incomplete details

a)  Illegible handwriting

12.    **Do the entries in your passbook contain errors?**
       a. Yes     b. No
If yes how many times did you point out to the bank an error in your passbook entries during the last 12 months? _____ times

13.    **Due you have any term deposit with this bank?**
       a. Yes     b. No
If yes, under what plan:

a)  _____

b)  _____

c)  _____

14. **Do you receive any intimations from the branch before the FD matures?**

    a. Yes      b. No

15. **How much time does the bank take to**

    a) Issue/Renew a FD receipt _____mts.

    b) Encash a FD receipt _____ mts.

16. **Did you ever apply for loan against your FDR.**

    a. Yes      b. No

    If yes how long did it take to receive the amount? _____ days

17. **Have you had an occasion to send remittance through**

                                                  Yes            No

    a) Demand draft

    b) Telegraphic transfer

    c) Mail transfer

18. **How much time did it take (or does it usually take the case of more frequent experiences) to purchase a DD at this branch _____mts.**

19. **How much time did it take for the other party receive the remittance in case of**

    a) MT _____days

    b) TT _____days

20. **Has the remittance effected correctly?**

    a. Yes      b. No

    Have you had an occasion to encash a bank draft at a branch where you do not have an account?

    a. Yes      b. No

21. **Are you a bank borrower through this bank?**

a. Yes  b. No

22. **If yes, what type of credit facilities do you currently enjoy with this bank?**

| Type of facility | For the last how many years | Nature of security |
|---|---|---|
| Loan | | |
| Cash credit | | |
| Overdraft | | |
| Bills | | |
| Any other facilities | | |

Code for security given for:

(a) Pledge/Hypothecation of stocks/Machinery/book debts

(b) Mortgage of immovables

(c) Shares

(d) LIC policy

(e) FDR

(f) Gold ornaments

(g) Bills

(h) Any other

23. **Please indicate the time taken in days by various stages in respect of your recent loan proposal?**

24. **Did you find the procedures cumbersome?**

a. Yes  b. No

25. **Was it necessary on your part to use some influence at any stage to facilitate availability of credit?**

a. Yes  b. No

**26.** **If YES, please indicate so**

                                                         Yes          No

    (a) Using intermediary or consultancy services

    (b) Applying political influence

    (c) Approaching through bank staff or executive

    (d) Any other (Please state)        _____

**27.** **Did you find any information asked by the branch/bank while processing your loan application, unnecessary, not available or too confidential to part with?**
    a. Yes    b. No

**28.** **If YES. please specify terms of information called for which were**
    a)  Unavailable
    b)  Confidential
    c)  Unnecessary

**29.** **Could you understand the implications of the documents executed by you with the bank in respect of your credit facility?**

    a. Yes    b. No

**30.** **Indicate the approximate number of signature/ initials you had to put on documents for getting the credit facility.**

    a)  Less than 10

    b)  More than 10

**31.** **Do you have a personal experience of:**

                                                         Yes          No

    a)  Loss of draft

    b)  Loss of FDR

    c)  Cancellation of a draft

    d)  Claiming balance in the account of a deceased person

    e)  Encashment of term deposit before maturity

f) Opening an account which has not been operated for a long period

If YES, what had been your experience?

g) Satisfactory

h) Unsatisfactory

32. **Do you consider the charges levied by the bank for providing the following services reasonable?**

Yes    No

a) Collection of outstanding cheque

b) Remittances

c) Issue of DD

d) Safe deposit lockers

e) Safe custody

f) Services to current deposit account holders

33. **Did you avail of any other services offered by the bank such as travellers' cheque, gift cheque, safe deposit lockers etc?**

a. Yes    b. No

If YES, do you think the services provided to you were?

a) Satisfactory

b) Unsatisfactory

34. **Do you have the experience of dealing with any foreign bank (as a customer operating an account)?**

a. Yes    b. No

If YES, please state the name _____

35. **Do you think that services rendered by this bank as compared to foreign bank are**

Yes    No

a) Better

b) Just the same

c) Not good

d) Can't say

36. **As a customer of the branch, what is your general impression about the services you are getting from the branch?**

                                              Yes                  No

a) very good

b) Good

c) Unsatisfactory

37. **Physical comforts provided for the customer while waiting in the branch are:**

                                              Yes                  No

a) Better

b) Fair

c) Poor

38. **Do you find the bank staff working as a team to meet your needs as a customer?**

                                              Yes                  No

a) Most of the times

b) Sometimes

c) Not at all

39. **How do you find the attitude of staff members towards the customers at the branch?**

| | Most of the times | Sometimes | Never |
|---|---|---|---|
| a. They are receptive to customers enquiry | | | |
| b. They are helpful and cooperative | | | |
| c. They are prompt and quick in attending to customer's needs | | | |

d. They are polite and
   courteous in responding

e.   They are willing to go out of
     the way to meet any special
     needs of the customer when
     they arise.

40.   **In respect of your dealing with the branch did you experience any of the following situations.**

                                                    Yes        No

a.   Inadequate knowledge of the staff

b.   Negligence on the part of the staff

c.   Delay in getting your transaction completed
     due to lengthy-procedures

41.   **Whenever unsatisfied with the service of the bank, what did you do?**

                                          Yes              No

   a)   Did not make any complaint.

   b)   Verbally complained to the Manager

   c)   Submitted a written complaint to the
        Branch Manager

42.   **What was the reason for the complaint?**

                                       Yes            No

   a)   Error or mistake in transaction

   b)   Avoidable delay in service

   c)   Misbehaviour or rudeness on the part of the staff

   d)   Any other reason, please mention_____

43.   **During the last one year or so were there any situations when you were not satisfied by some services rendered by this bank and felt like complaining?**

        a. Yes        b. No

**44.**   **In regard to your complaint, what was the response from the bank?**

   a) Satisfactory

   b) Unsatisfactory

**45.**   **Does the branch manager/staff at the branch take initiative in giving you advice with regard to:**

                                          Strongly agree      Agree

   a)   Choice of deposit plan

   b)   Mode of operating accounts

   c)   Choice or borrowing facilities

   d)   Other services

**46.**   **In correspondence with you ,is your bank**

                                   Yes          No

   a)   Prompt

   b)   Helpful

   c)   Polite

**47.**   **To meet growing customer needs, many banks have introduced some of the following facilities/services. What do you think of the following services provided by your bank?**

                            Satisfactory     Unsatisfactory

   a)   Loan linked deposit

   b)   Credit cards

   c)   Travellers' cheque

   d)   Single window approach like teller system

   e)   Specialized branches for SSI/ industrial
        advance/ savings bank

   f)   Installation of ATM operating 24 hours

**48.**   **Any other services would you like to avail from your bank?**

   a. Yes      b. No

49.  Would you like to make any other suggestions which would enable the bank to serve you better?

  a. Yes       b. No

  If YES, please state your suggestion

50.  How do you find services provided by your bank today in comparison with its service earlier?

                        Yes         No      Not Sure
  a)  A lot of improvement

  b)  Little improvement

  c)  No improvement at all

  d)  Going bad

51.  Do you think that Internet book keeping and record maintenance through computers would increase banks efficiency and improve customer service?

                        Yes            No          Can't say

52.  At present, electronic fund transfer and electronic clearing system are gaining momentum. Is it safe in your opinion?

                        Yes            No          Can't say

53.  Do you think that the incidence of crimes and robberies are on an increase in nationalized banks?

                        Yes            No          Can't say

54.  Do you think that frauds and cases of cheating, forgeries, manipulation of cheques ,drafts etc., are also on the increase in nationalized banks?

                        Yes            No          Can't say

55.  Do you think that nationalized banks today are ready to meet challenges/threat of privatization, liberalization and globalization and the impact of information technology?

56.  Some of the banks are converting their ATM cards to debit cards compulsorily and levy charges. Do you think such a system should be present?

Yes            No            Can't say

**57.    Do you face any problem with regard to foreign currency remittances?**

Yes            No            Can't say

a)  Transfer

b)  Deducting charges

c)  Processing time

d)  Withdrawal time

e)  Any other problem, please state_____

**58.    Which private banks and foreign banks factors/services/facilities according to you are affecting nationalized banks?**

a)  ATM banking and computerization

b)  ECS and EFT

c)  Internet banking/mobile banking

d)  Debit cards/credit cards

e)  Loans

f)  Any other_____

**59.    Would you like to suggest any innovative change in product or service to enhance customer satisfaction in future?**

a. Yes        b. No

**60.    How would you compare this bank with a foreign bank?**

Satisfactory        Not satisfactory

a)  Services being offered

b)  Processing time

c)  Electronic banking/computerization

d)  Accuracy in providing information

# Appendix II

# Reference Books

| | |
|---|---|
| Zikmund W.G, Babin B.J | Marketing Research : Cengage Learning India Pvt. Ltd., 418 FIE Patpargarj, Delhi-110092 (2007) |
| Suja R. Nair | Marketing Research : Himalaya Publishing House Pvt. Ltd., Mumbai-400004 (2012) |
| Malhotra N.K, Dash Satyabhuson | Marketing Research- An Applied Orientation : Dorling Kindersley (India) Pvt. Ltd. (Pearson, Noida 201309) (2011) |
| David J. Luck, Hugh G. Wales, Donald A. Taylor, Ronald S. Rubin | Marketing Research : Prentice Hall of India Pvt. Ltd., New Delhi-110001 (1982) |
| Paul E. Green, Donald S. Tull, Gerald Albaum | Research for Marketing decisions : Prentice Hall of India Pvt. Ltd., New Delhi-110001 (2004) |
| Henry D | Road to Brand Equity : Himalaya Publishing House Pvt. Ltd., Mumbai-400004 (2004) |
| Goel B.S | Marketing Research : PragatiPrakashan, Meerut-250001 |
| Panneerselvam R | Research Methodology : Prentice Hall of India Pvt. Ltd., New Delhi-110001 (2005) |
| Rao A.B | Research Methodology for Management and Social Sciences : Excel Books, New Delhi-110028 (2008) |
| Bellur V. V | Marketing Research- Theory and Practice : Himalaya Publishing House Pvt. Ltd., Mumbai-400004 (1987) |

| | |
|---|---|
| Donald S. Tull, Del I. Hawkins | Marketing Research- Measurement and method : PHI Learning Pvt. Ltd., New Delhi-110001 (2009) |
| Beri G C | Marketing Research : Tata McGraw-Hill Publishing Co. Ltd, New Delhi (2000) |
| RajendraNargundkar | Marketing Research- Text and Cases : Tata McGraw-Hill Publishing Co. Ltd, New Delhi (2000) |
| Gupta S L | Marketing Research : Excel Books, New Delhi (1999) |
| Gupta P. K | Marketing Management and Research : Everest Publishing House, Pune (1999) |

# Appendix III

# Statistical Table

## Table1 - Areas of a standard normal distribution

An entry in the table is the proportion under the entire curve which is between 1 = 0 and a positive value of z. Areas for negative values for z are obtained by symmetry.

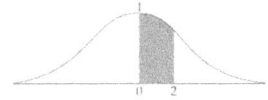

| X | .0 | .0.01 | .02 | .03 | .04 | .05 | .06 | .07 | .08 | .09 |
|---|---|---|---|---|---|---|---|---|---|---|
| .0 | .0000 | .0040 | .0080 | .0120 | .0160 | .0199 | .0239 | .0279 | .0319 | .0359 |
| .1 | .0398 | .0438 | .0478 | .0517 | .0557 | .0596 | .0636 | .0675 | .0714 | .0753 |
| .2 | .0793 | .0832 | .0871 | .0910 | .0948 | .0987 | .1026 | .1064 | .1103 | .1141 |
| .3 | .1179 | .1217 | .1255 | .1293 | .1331 | .1368 | .1406 | .1443 | .1480 | .1517 |
| .4 | .1554 | .1591 | .1628 | .1664 | .1700 | .1736 | .1772 | .1808 | .1844 | .1879 |
| 5 | .1915 | .1950 | .1985 | .2019 | .2054 | .2088 | .2123 | .2157 | .2190 | .2224 |
| .6 | .2257 | .2291 | .2324 | .2357 | .2389 | .2422 | .2454 | .2486 | .2517 | .2549 |
| .7 | .2580 | .2611 | .2642 | .2673 | .2903 | .2734 | .2764 | .2794 | .2823 | .2852 |
| .8 | .2881 | .2910 | .2939 | .2967 | .2995 | .3023 | .3051 | .3078 | .3106 | .3133 |
| .9 | .3159 | .3186 | .3212 | .3238 | .3264 | .3289 | .3315 | .3340 | .3365 | .3389 |
| 1.0 | .3413 | .3438 | .3461 | .3485 | .3508 | .3531 | .3354 | .3577 | .3599 | .3621 |
| 1.1 | .3643 | .3665 | .3686 | .3708 | .3729 | .3749 | .3770 | .3790 | .3810 | .3830 |
| 1.2 | .3849 | .3869 | .3888 | .3907 | .3925 | .3944 | .3962 | .3988 | .3997 | .4015 |
| 1.3 | .4032 | .4049 | .4066 | .4082 | .4099 | .4115 | .4131 | .4147 | .4162 | .4177 |
| 1.4 | .4192 | .4207 | .4222 | .4236 | .4251 | .4265 | .4279 | .4292 | .4306 | .4319 |
| 1.5 | .4332 | .4345 | .4357 | .4370 | .4382 | .4394 | .4406 | .4418 | .4429 | .4441 |
| 1.6 | .4452 | .4463 | .4474 | .4484 | .4495 | .4505 | .4515 | .4525 | .4535 | .4545 |
| 1.7 | .4554 | .4564 | .4573 | .4582 | .4591 | .4599 | .4608 | .4616 | .4625 | .4633 |
| 1.8 | .4641 | .4649 | .4656 | .4664 | .4671 | .4678 | .4686 | .4693 | .4699 | .4706 |
| 1.9 | .4713 | .4719 | .4726 | .4732 | .4738 | .4744 | .4750 | .4756 | .4761 | .4767 |
| 2.0 | .4772 | .4778 | .4783 | .4788 | .4793 | .4798 | .4803 | .4808 | .4812 | .4817 |
| 2.1 | .4821 | .4826 | .4830 | .4834 | .4838 | .4842 | .4846 | .4850 | .4854 | .4857 |
| 2.2 | .4851 | .4864 | .4868 | .4871 | .4875 | .4878 | .4881 | .4884 | .4887 | .4890 |
| 2.3 | .4893 | .4896 | .4898 | .4901 | .4904 | .4906 | .4909 | .4911 | .4913 | .4916 |
| 2.4 | .4918 | .4920 | .4922 | .4925 | .4927 | .4929 | .4931 | .4932 | .4934 | .4936 |
| 2.5 | .4938 | .4940 | .4941 | .4943 | .4945 | .4946 | .4948 | .4949 | .4951 | .4952 |
| 2.6 | .4953 | .4955 | .4956 | .4957 | .4959 | .4960 | .4961 | .4962 | .4963 | .4964 |
| 2.7 | .4965 | .4966 | .4967 | .4968 | .4969 | .4970 | .4971 | .4972 | .4973 | .4974 |
| 2.8 | .4974 | .4975 | .4976 | .4977 | .4977 | .4978 | .4979 | .4979 | .4980 | .4981 |
| 2.9 | .4981 | .4982 | .4982 | .4983 | .4984 | .4984 | .4985 | .4985 | .4986 | .4986 |
| 3.0 | .4987 | .4987 | .4987 | .4988 | .4988 | .4989 | .4989 | .4989 | .4990 | .4990 |

## Table 2 – Critical Values of student's Distribution

| d.f. | Level of significance for two – tailed test | | | | | d.f. |
|---|---|---|---|---|---|---|
| | 0.20 | 0.10 | 0.05 | 0.02 | 0.01 | |
| | Level of significance for one – tailed test | | | | | |
| | 0.10 | 0.05 | 0.025 | 0.01 | 0.005 | |
| 1 | 3.078 | 6.314 | 12.706 | 31.821 | 63.657 | 1 |
| 2 | 1.886 | 2.920 | 4.303 | 6.965 | 9.925 | 2 |
| 3 | 1.638 | 2.353 | 3.182 | 4.541 | 5.841 | 3 |
| 4 | 1.533 | 2.132 | 2.776 | 3.747 | 4.604 | 4 |
| 5 | 1.476 | 2.015 | 2.571 | 3.365 | 4.032 | 5 |
| 6 | 1.440 | 1.943 | 2.447 | 3.143 | 3.707 | 6 |
| 7 | 1.415 | 1.895 | 2.365 | 2.998 | 3.499 | 7 |
| 8 | 1.397 | 1.860 | 2.306 | 2.896 | 3.355 | 8 |
| 9 | 1.383 | 1.833 | 2.262 | 2.821 | 3.250 | 9 |
| 10 | 1.372 | 1.812 | 2.228 | 2.764 | 3.169 | 10 |
| 11 | 1.363 | 1.796 | 2.201 | 2.718 | 3.106 | 11 |
| 12 | 1.356 | 1.782 | 2.179 | 2.681 | 3.055 | 12 |
| 13 | 1.350 | 1.771 | 2.160 | 2.650 | 3.012 | 13 |
| 14 | 1.345 | 1.761 | 2.145 | 2.624 | 2.977 | 14 |
| 15 | 1.341 | 1.753 | 2.731 | 2.602 | 2.947 | 15 |
| 16 | 1.337 | 1.746 | 2.120 | 2.583 | 2.921 | 16 |
| 17 | 1.333 | 1.740 | 2.110 | 2.567 | 2.898 | 17 |
| 18 | 1.330 | 1.734 | 2.101 | 2.552 | 2.878 | 18 |
| 19 | 1.328 | 1.729 | 2.093 | 2.539 | 2.861 | 19 |
| 20 | 1.325 | 1.725 | 2.086 | 2.528 | 2.845 | 20 |
| 21 | 1.323 | 1.721 | 2.080 | 2.518 | 2.831 | 21 |
| 22 | 1.321 | 1.717 | 2.074 | 2.508 | 2.819 | 22 |
| 23 | 1.319 | 1.714 | 2.069 | 2.500 | 2.807 | 23 |
| 24 | 1.318 | 1.711 | 2.064 | 2.492 | 2.797 | 24 |
| 25 | 1.316 | 1.708 | 2.060 | 2.485 | 2.787 | 25 |
| 26 | 1.315 | 1.706 | 2.056 | 2.479 | 2.779 | 26 |
| 27 | 1.314 | 1.703 | 2.052 | 2.473 | 2.771 | 27 |
| 28 | 1.313 | 1.701 | 2.048 | 2.467 | 2.763 | 28 |
| 29 | 1.311 | 1.699 | 2.045 | 2.462 | 2.756 | 29 |
| Infinity | 1.282 | 1.645 | 1.960 | 2.326 | 2.576 | Infinity |

Table 3 – Critical Values of X³

| Degrees of freedom | Probability under H₀ that $X^2$ > chi square | | | | | | |
|---|---|---|---|---|---|---|---|
| | .99 | .95 | .50 | .10 | .05 | .02 | .01 |
| 1 | .000157 | .00393 | .455 | 2.706 | 3.841 | 5.412 | 6.635 |
| 2 | .0201 | .103 | 1.386 | 4.605 | 5.991 | 7.824 | 9.210 |
| 3 | .115 | .352 | 2.366 | 6.251 | 7.815 | 9.837 | 11.341 |
| 4 | .297 | .711 | 3.357 | 7.779 | 9.488 | 11.668 | 13.277 |
| 5 | .554 | .1145 | 4.351 | 9.236 | 11.070 | 13.388 | 15.086 |
| 6 | .872 | 1.635 | 5.348 | 10.645 | 12.592 | 15.033 | 16.812 |
| 7 | 1.239 | 2.167 | 6.346 | 12.017 | 14.067 | 16.622 | 18.475 |
| 8 | 1.646 | 2.733 | 7.344 | 13.362 | 15.507 | 18.168 | 20.090 |
| 9 | 2.088 | 3.325 | 8.343 | 14.684 | 16.919 | 19.679 | 21.666 |
| 10 | 2.558 | 3.940 | 9.342 | 15.987 | 18.307 | 21.161 | 23.209 |
| 11 | 3.053 | 4.575 | 10.341 | 17.275 | 19.675 | 22.618 | 24.725 |
| 12 | 3.571 | 5.226 | 11.340 | 18.549 | 21.026 | 23.054 | 26.217 |
| 13 | 4.107 | 5.892 | 12.340 | 19.812 | 22.362 | 25.472 | 72.688 |
| 14 | 4.660 | 6.571 | 13.339 | 21.064 | 23.685 | 26.873 | 29.141 |
| 15 | 4.229 | 7.261 | 14.339 | 22.307 | 24.996 | 28.259 | 30.578 |
| 16 | 5.812 | 7.962 | 15.338 | 23.542 | 26.292 | 29.633 | 32.000 |
| 17 | 6.408 | 8.672 | 16.538 | 24.769 | 27.587 | 30.995 | 33.409 |
| 18 | 7.015 | 9.390 | 17.338 | 25.989 | 28.869 | 32.346 | 34.805 |
| 19 | 7.633 | 10.117 | 18.338 | 27.204 | 30.144 | 33.687 | 36.191 |
| 20 | 8.260 | 10.851 | 19.337 | 28.412 | 31.410 | 35.020 | 37.566 |
| 21 | 8.897 | 11.591 | 20.337 | 29.615 | 32.671 | 36.343 | 38.932 |
| 22 | 9.542 | 12.338 | 21.337 | 30.813 | 33.924 | 37.659 | 40.289 |
| 23 | 10.196 | 13.091 | 22.337 | 32.007 | 35.172 | 38.968 | 41.638 |
| 24 | 10.856 | 13.848 | 23.337 | 32.196 | 36.415 | 40.270 | 42.980 |
| 25 | 11.524 | 14.611 | 24.337 | 34.382 | 37.652 | 41.566 | 44.314 |
| 26 | 12.198 | 15.379 | 25.336 | 35.363 | 38.885 | 41.856 | 45.642 |
| 27 | 12.879 | 16.151 | 26.336 | 36.741 | 40.113 | 44.140 | 46.963 |
| 28 | 13.565 | 16.928 | 27.336 | 37.916 | 41.337 | 45.419 | 48.278 |
| 29 | 14.256 | 17.708 | 28.336 | 39.087 | 42.557 | 46.693 | 49.588 |
| 30 | 14.953 | 18.493 | 29.336 | 40.256 | 43.773 | 47.962 | 50.892 |

Note : For degrees of freedom greater than 30, the quantity $2X^2 - \sqrt{2\,d.f.-1}$ may be used as a normal variate with unit cariance i.e., y= $\sqrt{2X^2} - \sqrt{2\,d.f.-1}$ .

Table 4(a) – Critical values of F-Distribution

## (at 5 percent)

| $v_1$ \ $v$ | 1 | 2 | 3 | 4 | 5 | 6 | 8 | 12 | 24 | |
|---|---|---|---|---|---|---|---|---|---|---|
| 1 | 161.4 | 199.5 | 215.7 | 224.6 | 230.2 | 234.0 | 238.9 | 243.9 | 249.1 | 243.3 |
| 2 | 18.51 | 19.00 | 19.16 | 19.25 | 19.30 | 19.33 | 19.37 | 19.41 | 19.45 | 16.50 |
| 3 | 10.13 | 9.55 | 9.28 | 9.12 | 9.01 | 8.94 | 8.85 | 8.74 | 8.64 | 8.53 |
| 4 | 7.71 | 6.94 | 6.59 | 6.39 | 6.26 | 6.16 | 6.04 | 5.91 | 5.77 | 5.63 |
| 5 | 6.61 | 5.79 | 5.41 | 5.19 | 5.05 | 4.95 | 4.82 | 4.68 | 4.53 | 4.36 |
| 6 | 5.99 | 5.14 | 4.76 | 4.53 | 4.39 | 4.28 | 4.15 | 4.00 | 3.84 | 3.67 |
| 7 | 5.59 | 4.74 | 4.35 | 4.12 | 3.97 | 3.87 | 3.73 | 3.57 | 3.41 | 3.23 |
| 8 | 5.32 | 4.46 | 4.07 | 3.84 | 3.69 | 3.58 | 3.44 | 3.28 | 3.12 | 2.93 |
| 9 | 5.12 | 4.26 | 3.86 | 3.63 | 3.48 | 3.37 | 3.23 | 3.07 | 2.90 | 2.71 |
| 10 | 4.96 | 4.10 | 3.71 | 3.48 | 3.33 | 3.22 | 3.07 | 2.91 | 2.74 | 2.54 |
| 11 | 4.84 | 3.98 | 3.59 | 3.36 | 3.20 | 3.09 | 2.95 | 2.79 | 2.61 | 2.40 |
| 12 | 4.75 | 3.88 | 3.49 | 3.26 | 3.11 | 3.00 | 2.85 | 2.69 | 2.51 | 2.30 |
| 13 | 4.67 | 3.80 | 3.41 | 3.18 | 3.02 | 2.92 | 2.77 | 2.60 | 2.42 | 2.21 |
| 14 | 4.60 | 3.74 | 3.34 | 3.11 | 2.96 | 2.85 | 2.70 | 2.53 | 2.35 | 2.13 |
| 15 | 4.54 | 3.68 | 3.29 | 3.6 | 2.90 | 2.79 | 2.64 | 2.48 | 2.29 | 2.07 |
| 16 | 4.49 | 3.63 | 3.24 | 3.01 | 2.85 | 2.74 | 2.59 | 2.42 | 2.24 | 2.01 |
| 17 | 4.45 | 3.59 | 3.20 | 2.96 | 2.81 | 2.70 | 2.55 | 2.38 | 2.19 | 1.96 |
| 18 | 4.41 | 3.55 | 3.16 | 2.93 | 2.77 | 2.66 | 2.51 | 2.34 | 2.15 | 1.92 |
| 19 | 4.38 | 3.52 | 3.13 | 2.90 | 2.74 | 2.63 | 2.48 | 2.31 | 2.11 | 1.88 |
| 20 | 4.35 | 3.49 | 3.10 | 2.87 | 2.71 | 2.60 | 2.45 | 2.28 | 2.08 | 1.84 |
| 21 | 4.32 | 3.47 | 3.07 | 2.84 | 2.68 | 2.57 | 2.42 | 2.25 | 2.05 | 1.81 |
| 22 | 4.30 | 3.44 | 3.05 | 2.82 | 2.66 | 2.55 | 2.40 | 2.23 | 2.03 | 1.78 |
| 23 | 4.28 | 3.42 | 3.03 | 2.80 | 2.64 | 2.53 | 2.38 | 2.20 | 2.01 | 1.76 |
| 24 | 4.26 | 3.40 | 3.01 | 2.78 | 2.62 | 2.51 | 2.36 | 2.18 | 1.98 | 1.73 |
| 25 | 4.24 | 3.338 | 2.99 | 2.76 | 2.60 | 2.49 | 2.34 | 2.16 | 1.96 | 1.71 |
| 26 | 4.22 | 3.37 | 2.98 | 2.74 | 2.59 | 2.47 | 2.32 | 2.15 | 1.95 | 1.69 |
| 27 | 4.21 | 3.35 | 2.96 | 2.73 | 2.57 | 2.46 | 2.31 | 2.13 | 1.93 | 1.67 |
| 28 | 4.20 | 3.34 | 2.95 | 2.71 | 2.56 | 2.45 | 2.29 | 2.12 | 1.91 | 1.65 |
| 29 | 4.18 | 3.33 | 2.93 | 2.70 | 2.54 | 2.43 | 2.28 | 2.10 | 1.90 | 1.64 |
| 30 | 4.17 | 3.32 | 2.92 | 2.69 | 2.53 | 2.42 | 2.27 | 2.09 | 1.89 | 1.62 |
| 40 | 408 | 3.23 | 2.84 | 2.61 | 2.45 | 2.34 | 2.18 | 2.00 | 1.79 | 1.51 |
| 60 | 4.00 | 3.15 | 2.76 | 2.52 | 2.37 | 2.25 | 2.10 | 1.92 | 1.70 | 1.39 |
| 120 | 3.92 | 3.07 | 2.68 | 2.45 | 2.29 | 2.17 | 2.02 | 1.83 | 1.61 | 1.25 |
| 00 | 3.84 | 2.99 | 2.60 | 2.37 | 2.21 | 2.10 | 1.94 | 1.75 | 1.52 | 1.00 |

$V_1$: Degrees of freedom for greater variance.
$V_2$: Degrees of freedom for smaller variance.

www.ingramcontent.com/pod-product-compliance
Lightning Source LLC
Chambersburg PA
CBHW061127210326
41518CB00034B/2531